Cultural Rights and Justice

John Clammer

Cultural Rights and Justice

Sustainable Development, the Arts and the Body

palgrave
macmillan

John Clammer
O.P. Jindal Global University
Sonipat, India

ISBN 978-981-13-2810-7 ISBN 978-981-13-2811-4 (eBook)
https://doi.org/10.1007/978-981-13-2811-4

Library of Congress Control Number: 2018962357

Cover credit: Jethuynh

This Palgrave Macmillan imprint is published by the registered company Springer Nature Singapore Pte Ltd.
The registered company address is: 152 Beach Road, #21-01/04 Gateway East, Singapore 189721, Singapore

For Miyoko
In troubled times, one who has brought so much beauty into my life

Contents

CHAPTER 1

Culture, Development and Cultural Rights

The notion of human rights, even when more honored in the breach than in practice, is now an established part of the architecture of the international order. Since its conception in 1948, in the wake of a devastating world war and at the beginning of an era marked by optimism about the prospects of "development" for a world undergoing reconstruction and with decolonization in rapid progress globally, the foundational document—the Universal Declaration of Human Rights—has undergone both challenges and extensions. The former largely relate to the question of the genuine universality of the Declaration, one drafted at a time when the newly created United Nations Organization had few members, and which, as subsequent debate has noted, embodied essentially Western philosophical concepts about such issues as the rights of individuals in relation to the rights of communities, and as such did not fully represent or reflect cultural diversity and the sources from which notions of rights have often emerged, such as religions. The latter relate both to the silences of the originating document—in particular questions of cultural and economic rights, and to issues that have emerged in the rapidly transforming world since the late 1940s in which a huge range of issues unsuspected at the time have emerged. These include questions of new technology, medical ethics, trade, nuclear power, environment, new categories of refugees, access to and exploitation of space, the seas and unpopulated areas such as Antarctica, potentially rich in mineral resources, the rights of children, protection of minorities and even such issues quite

J. Clammer, *Cultural Rights and Justice*,
https://doi.org/10.1007/978-981-13-2811-4_1

beyond the scope of any declaration of purely *human* rights, such as the rights (if such there be) of animals and of the biosphere in general.

The context of the Declaration is significant here—the hope not only to avoid the repeated trauma of future wars which, with the advent of nuclear weapons, could only be immensely more devastating that the one just terminated, but that, with colonization ending, initiatives such as the Marshall Plan working successfully to rebuild a war-shattered Europe, the economic crises of the Great Depression now receding into the past, and with new technologies available (many paradoxically developed during the pressures of the war) that could be turned to socially productive ends, a new era of peace and development was dawning. Indeed, the very notion of "development" as a purposeful and directed policy of interventions, particularly in the "Third World" (largely the former colonies and those just emerging from colonial rule), aimed at the eradication of poverty, the promotion of (Western style) democracy and a push toward industrialization and "modernization" (of health systems, education, courts and so forth), is seen as emerging precisely at this time. Of course perceptive critics soon arose to argue (and still do—see Sachs 1995) that the whole project of development was simply a disguised form of Westernization, and to a great extent a political rather than a humanitarian project (especially as the Cold War got underway), and even that it represented colonialism by another name. As the notion of globalization has become a framing concept for the current planet-wide processes of integration (in the interests of some), much the same critique has been extended to that too, to the extent that in the view of many on what remains of the traditional Left, neo-liberal capitalism, globalization and development are more or less synonyms. Be that as it may, it is important to note the original coincidence of the idea of universal human rights and the idea of development, at least as it was conceived in the 1940s and 1950s. This is an idea that, while it has never been totally lost, is no longer a dominant trope in development discourse.

The original declaration has undergone many extensions, embodied in such instruments as the International Covenant on Civil and Political Rights and the International Covenant on Economic, Social and Cultural Rights (both approved by the UN General Assembly in 1966), and specific declarations of the rights of children, of refugees, of minorities, indigenous peoples and other vulnerable groups emanating from International Labor Organization (ILO) and very much from UNESCO which has a long history of passing such declarations, up to an including the major Convention on the Protection and Promotion of the Diversity of Cultural Expressions in 2005 (for an extended discussion of this latter document see De Beukelaer et al. 2015). Significant among these has been the recognition that human rights encompass and imply *cultural* rights, yet while this is true, the notion of such rights and what they may in turn encompass, is still underdeveloped. In the pages that follow several issues relating to this will be addressed: the meaning of the term "cultural rights", its connection to other forms of rights, its concrete expression in a variety of cultural manifestations and very centrally, the links between cultural rights and what here and elsewhere (Clammer 2012) I have called "holistic development"—forms of development that far exceed the purely economic or material and involve the development *of* culture, the pursuit of social and cultural justice, concern for the environment as the essential context for the maintenance and flourishing of both human and non-human life forms and ideas of both material and cultural sustainability and the links between all of these. The very notion of "rights" implies an *ethical* discourse, and this aspect of discussion of rights needs to be drawn out and strengthened, and linked to a range of significant debates—in the somewhat underdeveloped field of development ethics, to the rapidly emerging field of environmental ethics, to the rights (including cultural rights) of refugees, migrants and minorities, to gender, and to the uncomfortable but essential debate of the *quality* of culture, and whether a debate can be initiated about the destructive, trivializing and negative aspects of much of our contemporary culture, as well as to its constructive and socially positive dimensions.

If one jumps ahead from history to the present moment, it is evident that the sources of most of our current planetary crisis (conflict, climate change, resource depletion, pollution, loss of biodiversity and so forth) are traceable directly to our cultural habits—over consumption, addiction to the car, the plane and the long-distance transportation of commodities, a throwaway habit, lack of recycling, addiction to novelty in fashion, furnishings and housing and cradle-to-grave design, rather than cradle-to-cradle. Both lack of sustainability and the difficulties of making a transition to a sustainable society are cultural, not natural (Clammer 2016), and if this is the case, then solutions must lay in changes of cultural values (including in the largely socially produced structure of our desires) and behavior. But this is where the question of cultural rights becomes complex. Let us start with a working definition: that cultural rights are the right to a culture, to cultural expression, to the free development of that culture from which one derives one's primary identity and to the right to defend that culture against its destruction or erosion. In a sense, of course, everyone "has" a culture: it is part of the definition of being human. The problem is the negation or diminution of the forms of cultural expression (foods, language, dress, religion, housing styles, music, literature, dance, livelihoods) from which one derives a sense of identity and allows one to say with confidence that "I am an x". Cultures can be threatened politically, by globalization and the homogenization that it so often produces, by colonization, and even by technological advances such as the Internet, where most of the content is in a very limited range of "major" metropolitan languages, and especially English. Loss of cultural diversity (often signaled by the disappearance of languages) is in many ways parallel to the loss of biodiversity, and indeed is implicated in it in so far as many indigenous languages embody a huge amount of ecological knowledge, which is lost with the vanishing of any one of those languages from the total repertoire of the world's linguistic heritage. The right to possess a culture and the dignity that it confers (including an identity and a history) is thus a fundamental human right, the loss of which not only diminishes the variety and complexity of the world, but potentially endangers our future as a species, as vital and hard-won knowledge is destroyed or denigrated and as ways of life and forms of experience are pushed into extinction.

Cultural Diversity and Cultural Rights

International bodies concerned with culture, and in particular UNESCO, have devoted considerable attention to some of these issues, including the dangers of the loss of cultural diversity and the need to protect local cultures from erosion, particularly by the forces of globalization. Such major instruments include the UNESCO Convention on the Protection and Promotion of the Diversity of Cultural Expressions (2005) mentioned above, and the 2001 Universal Declaration on Cultural Diversity, which opens with the words "Committed to the full implementation of the human rights and fundamental freedoms proclaimed in the Universal Declaration of Human Rights" and continues in its preamble with the statement that "culture is at the heart of contemporary debates about identity, social cohesion, and the development of a knowledge-based economy".

But when the rather fuzzy UNESCO concept of culture used in these various declarations is broken down, it turns out to have very many dimensions, any one of which raises interesting questions about the application of an idea of cultural rights. Biopiracy—the utilization without consent of natural products long used by native peoples, and the conversion of them into profit-making products (typically pharmaceuticals) and attempting to patent them without payment of royalties—is a well-known and now well contested issue, one that sometimes overlaps with genetic manipulation and similar practices that involve both interference with natural processes and exploitation of local knowledge. Less acknowledged is the issue of intellectual and creative property rights. Where such knowledge is protected by formal patents or by agreements enforced by the World Intellectual Property Organization (WIPO), few problems arise. But where such knowledge is truly local and there is little or no awareness of or access to intellectual property protection, cultural piracy is easy. An important aspect of this relates to creative products such as music, crafts or theatre. When is it appropriate to "borrow" from another artistic tradition (as has indeed frequently happened in Western art, with for example the "discovery" in the late nineteenth and early twentieth centuries of Japanese art and of "primitive" art), and when does this become cultural appropriation? The hybrid nature of so much culture in the current globalized world situation makes this a difficult question to answer when Hollywood penetrates almost everywhere, where Japanese *manga* and *anime* are consumed all over the planet, where Singaporean teenagers listen to both British and Taiwanese pop music, where the shelves of Japanese video rental stores are filled with Korean soap operas and where McDonalds and Starbucks seem to appear wherever one travels, and most of us wear local Western fashions that have now become the global norm. Deliberate hybridization is now often typical of theatre in and beyond Asia, a phenomenon that greatly worries some critics such as the Indian writer and director Rustom Bharucha who sees the adoption of stories, styles and themes from South Asian classics by Western theatre directors as appropriation and hence as a kind of intellectual colonialism (Bharucha 1993).

These kinds of questions can be extended to a range of issues such as open source publishing (should all knowledge, especially that funded out of the public purse, such as in universities, be accessible to all without cost, or would this diminish the interest of scholars and researchers in carrying out original work? What are the limits (including the time limits) of copyright? Is censorship ever acceptable (especially when politically motivated) or does it, at least in some cases, protect the vulnerable (e.g. children) from exposure to harmful material? Can such an argument be extended to the arts? (Young 2005). Who, if anyone, is responsible for identifying and then protecting "heritage" or is such "heritage" simply old stuff, probably originally associated with a now discredited aristocracy ("stately homes")? Can much the same be said of "classical" music, "Old Master" paintings and most of the material to be found in museums and non-contemporary art galleries? (Anheier and Isar 2011; Hobsbawm 2014). It is easy to see why culture is rightly considered to be a site of struggle. Quite harmless seeming questions turn out to be loaded with controversy. Furthermore, the context in which such questions are raised is changing rapidly around us. Globalization and transnationalism have produced new and ever more volatile forms of hybridity, culture contact, points of conflict and points of sharing, especially as the media becomes less and less bound by the old national boundaries. Unprecedented numbers of people are on the move for a large variety of reasons—as refugees, tourists, professionals, business people, workers with NGOs and international organizations. Whether or not we have reached the point of "peak oil", a post-oil future is surely not far away and yet very little is being done politically, economically or culturally to prepare for it (Urry 2013). The Indian novelist and one—time anthropologist Amitav Ghosh has suggested in a significant recent book that climate change touches upon culture in at least three ways—as itself a culturally driven phenomenon, as a world-changing process that inexplicably has been little addressed by serious fiction writers, and as a challenge to evolve (rapidly) new forms of cultural expression to respond to it (Ghosh 2016). If, as Naomi Klein has suggested in the title of her powerful book on the subject of climate change "This Changes Everything", then indeed a profound cultural response is required (Klein 2015).

The field of "cultural studies" has become in many ways a sadly narcissistic form of intellectual endeavor more obsessed with such topics as fashion, bodybuilding, soap operas and pop art than it is with the huge and looming macro-issues that now confront us. It has, with the possible exception of postcolonial studies, shown no engagement with development studies, and has been largely silent on such key questions in social analysis as religion. Race, gender, visual studies and belatedly environment have appeared on its agenda, but these have not been for the most part systematically related to wider planetary problems, except through the already somewhat past the sell-by date lens of globalization studies. What does all this imply for an expanded conception of cultural rights? Several things, including most prominently, a clear understanding of what culture means in the contemporary world; a grasp of the rapidly evolving context in which culture now exists; the perception of a clear link between cultural rights and a holistic conception of development; and the necessity for an expanded conception of rights, understood as an ethical discourse, balanced by a conception of *responsibilities*, and one that extends beyond the purely human to the larger environment which itself provides the context in which all and any human cultures exist, and which sets unpassable limits on what is both desirable and possible.

The expansion of the concept of cultural rights has a number of consequences that spread across a number of dimensions. These include: bringing notions of cultural rights together with on-going debates about culture and development; in that context making the idea of culture *concrete*—citing that is, actual examples from art, performance and everyday life, in order to avoid both the highly abstract notion of culture that appears in so many debates of this nature, and to avoid identifying culture with social structure, as has happened in a great deal of the culture and development literature. It likewise includes bringing into discourse those areas of human experience largely neglected in development studies: religion, the emotions, embodiment, and very significantly, the *psychology* of social change and transformation and indeed the whole neglected field of political psychology (Nandy 1983, 1990). And it certainly involves the relationship between culture and economy. From all this emerge a number of practical steps—the consideration of *legal* steps to enhance and protect cultural rights, and the mechanisms for enforcing such protections, the role of education in promoting and internalizing rights in general, and consideration of the kinds of cultural activism that the pursuit of a widening circle of cultural rights might encourage, and the drawing of philosophy into the debate as both rights and development are recognized, as suggested above, as essentially *ethical* issues, as indeed are a wide range of contemporary questions including much major ones as climate change, poverty, the arms trade and trade practices in general, and of course the environment, issues until recently left largely outside of the repertoire of philosophical debate. At bottom indeed is a fundamental issue of philosophical anthropology—a conception of what human life should be like and the responsibilities of humans to their wider natural environment.

International law has not been silent on these issues, across a range of questions. These are represented in the number of legal instruments that now exist—documents such as the International Covenant on Economic, Social and Cultural Rights and its relationship to human rights in a broader sense (Craven 1995; Eide et al. 1995; High Commissioner for Human Rights 2005), the African Charter on Human and Peoples' Rights, the 2007 UN Declaration on the Rights of Indigenous Peoples (Thornberry 2002) among others. The perennial debate about the relationship of human rights to culture also continues as a central issue (Bell et al. 2001; An-Naim 1992) and the scope of the discourse constantly expands as more and more issues appear that fall within the scope of human and cultural rights debates—such as the cultural rights of refugees or internally displaced persons, the role and legal status of civil society organizations such as NGOs which frequently operate in a rights environment and/or promote agendas that promote either or both of human rights or specific forms of cultural freedom such as artistic freedom (Vickery 2018), or questions of sustainability and their consequences for social and cultural practices such as the reduction of consumption or giving up the car. We face in fact a rather paradoxical situation in that while international and national legal instruments exist for the promotion and protection of cultural rights in theory, in practice culture still tends to take the back seat when actual issues of development, politics or economics are at stake.

Cultural Rights and Social Justice

At the basis of the conception of cultural rights being advanced here is an equally expanded notion of social justice—one that considers not only the issues of economic equality, gender justice, access to education, health care, housing, legal protection and representation, but also the rights to leisure, cultural expression, a free emotional life, access to nature and aesthetic satisfactions, a spiritual life and the right to define identity as one wishes (a contested right that at the moment extends mostly to sexual identity). If one goes back and reads the old "human needs" literature of the 1980s, something that under the often pernicious impact of postmodernist and extreme deconstructionist thinking, dropped out of fashion, one finds in fact a not dissimilar notion—that for a flourishing existence, human beings do indeed have needs, and the space to exercise them and the resources to fulfill them. This idea has in many respects been reincarnated in the "capabilities" approach to development popularized in slightly different ways by Amartya Sen and Martha Nussbaum (Sen 2011; Nussbaum 2011), and extended by Nussbaum to the idea that active participation in cultural activities (many of them encapsulated under the term "the humanities") is not only desirable in itself, but is an essential prerequisite for democracy (Nussbaum 2012). History suggests that this is certainly true—many social movements being at base really cultural movements—struggles for recognition, the right to cultural expression and the overturning of cultural categories (such as gender or race) that have prevented freedom of expression and the access to cultural resources that should be the entitlement of all human beings. A very high percentage of suffering in the world is what Arthur Kleinman and collaborators have rightly termed "social suffering"—suffering produced by the very social processes and social structures that should ideally lead to emancipation and fulfillment (Kleinman et al. 1997). A natural corollary of any social constructivist approach to social reality (a position that seems to be very much in vogue at the moment) is that if we manufacture society and culture, we can change them. Analysis of cultural rights cannot stop at that point: it also requires action and transformation to ensure their fulfillment.

Discussion of the relationship between rights and culture is not in itself new: it has attracted a literature much of it generated by anthropologists who have in many cases encountered human rights abuses in the field and have as a consequence found it necessary to formulate a response, not only in immediate practical terms, but also in more theoretical ways, by engaging in the debate about the relationship between culture and rights, on-going since the original formulation of the (allegedly) Universal Declaration of Human Rights. These debates as a consequence have mainly centered on the problem of universality and the suspicion that the term, as used in the UDHR, is in fact shorthand for "Western Values" and certain liberal philosophical assumptions that underlay them, such as the preeminence of individualism. It is in relation to this that the subject of "Asian Values" has arisen, and which has focused attention not only on the universality issue, but also on the agendas of a number of Asian governments, wishing in practice not to open up a philosophical debate, but to suppress certain rights on the grounds, real or spurious, that they are not culturally acceptable in a given local context (Jacobsen and Bruun 2003). In national situations of multiculturalism and ethnic and religious diversity such as India real problems do indeed arise, such as the need for legal pluralism reflecting that diversity in which, for example, Muslim law (certainly in terms of such issues as divorce and the property rights of women) is not compatible with Hindu law in respect of the same issues, and in where the legal and cultural rights of other minorities, usually defined in religious terms (Christian, Jain, Sikh, Parsi, Jewish and so forth) also demand protection.

The empirical result of this is that cultural rights are not simply given, but have to be constantly struggled for and are almost always in a process of negotiation. Since culture itself is a constantly evolving and usually highly dynamic thing, this is to be expected. Hence the perpetual problems of even formulating an agreed definition as to what exactly it is. Indeed, it could be said that "cultural rights" and "culture" are virtually synonymous—every struggle to have a given cultural expression recognized as legitimate is at the same time a struggle for a cultural right. Such rights discourses have now also become globalized: in one sense the "local" no longer exists and the plight of refugees or migrants in one place does indeed become universalized (global media being one of the main factors behind this). Civil society entities, social movements, non-state actors of many kinds (including business) and "non-traditional" minorities struggling to emerge into a situation of recognition, dignity and legal protection, such as Gay and Lesbian movements, have all foregrounded the issue of culture. The notion of "multiculturalism" itself has consequently undergone transformation. It need no longer refer only to subcultures defined in an older anthropological sense (usually in terms of ethnicity, religion or geographical location), but also, as in the example just given, to emergent groups attempting to define themselves as such—still coming-into-being—and based on lifestyle preferences rather than traditional criteria of the kind that might be used to define a group in a census. The French sociologist Michel Maffesoli has argued that even such classical concepts as class are now eroding in the context of newly fluid and often transitory social structures and temporary arrangements, such that he prefers to refer to social units as "tribes"—ever shifting sets of allegiances based on consumption preferences and lifestyle and cultural choices, no longer defined by older patterns of social stratification or even income, and certainly not class (Maffesoli 1996). As the empirical aspects of culture change (under the impact of technology, globalization, internal evolution and creativity), so then will conceptions of rights;

the complex dialectic or interplay between them being an inherent and inescapable quality of the context, both theoretically and in terms of actual examples "on the ground" between culture and rights, and as international conventions evolve, and as groups no often at the point of disappearing, struggle to bring themselves back into existence by appealing to their ancient cultural characteristics, as, for example, with the Ainu people of northern Japan, many of whom are now, threatened by the erosion of their culture and assimilation into the mainstream Japanese society, are actively reconstructing "tradition", including very much its material forms such as wood carving, and very much the textile arts, the latter in particular also allowing for the cultural agency of women, since weaving and textile decoration are both ritually important and the domain of the female (Lewallen 2016).

This book then is not simply a *discussion* of the concept of cultural rights. It also attempts to *advance* it in the ways mentioned—by linking it more systematically to debates in development, to bringing ethics, rights, culture and development back into a more intimate dialogue with one another, toward cultivating a culture of peace by relating rights and peace studies, by foregrounding sources of values and meaning such as religion and by introducing into the debate a number of largely sidelined issues, such as the significance of memory for culture, the role of narratives and their power to create "new stories" through which new directions for our often self-destructive culture can be directed and the neglected role of the arts, all of which while, in some respects complicating the idea of cultural rights, also help to enrich it.

Rights then must be rooted in values, both local where these do not work against humanization or create inequalities and lack of access, and, in a different sense from that intended by the authors of the UDHR, universal. Today, all cultural rights must be rooted in our relationship to nature, and far from being a limitation, this creates the possibility not only of new or revised values, but of a form of harmony between what were at one time perceived as competing paradigms. A very good instance of this is in religion, where increasingly quite different traditions as diverse as Christianity, Islam, Buddhism and Shinto, are finding a common vocabulary in ecology and finding in this not only new ways of relating their traditional teachings to the world situation, but also new possibilities of interreligious dialogue (for a sampling of a rapidly proliferating literature see Gottlieb 2004, 2006). Development itself is not just a "technical" activity, important as that dimension certainly is, but one itself ultimately rooted in values—the kind of future society that we desire, its economic, political, social and cultural characteristics, in fact, in short, what we consider to be a good life. The analysis of cultural rights then necessitates the consideration of values, as both a philosophical and ethical issue as related to the goals and qualities of life, and in very practical terms as the basis for development policies and cultural policies (Clammer 1996). Since values cannot be separated from culture, the issues of the relationship between culture and rights, and of the barriers to intercultural communication, necessarily arise, not as a "one time" issue that can be settled so that we can "move on", but as an inherent part of the continuous evolution of cultures, changing planetary circumstances and expanding ethical paradigms (Clammer et al. 2004). The question of values intimately involves the nature of religion and religious cultures, an area very neglected in both culture and development discourses and in the analysis of cultural rights. In many societies throughout the world religion continues to play a highly significant role, and far from declining as the old secularization thesis predicted, has reemerged as a profound social, political and cultural force. Homi Bhabha years ago spoke of the neglect of the religious factor in terms of it being one of the "denied knowledges" (Bhabha 1994: 114), that, along with other forms of "indigenous knowledge", now needs to be very much recovered (Clammer 2009).

This suggests a number of ramifying questions and possibilities—a new and vital role for legal anthropology (Cowan et al. 2001; Wilson 1997), the fact that issues of culture are always political and so the pursuit of cultural rights must also involve political strategies, that the neglected (in relation to development studies) fields of cross-cultural psychology and of the psychology of change and innovation must be foregrounded, and that there must be a critical dimension to any discussion of values and culture. If it is our cultures that have got us into our current planet-wide crisis, then inevitably they must be critically examined, and where necessary, modified or discarded. The massive social and technological changes that have characterized recent decades have had multiple effects, many of which we do not even yet fully understand. These changes have produced unprecedented revolutions in culture, with corresponding shifts in subjectivities and identities, no longer necessarily expressed in the traditional categories of class, ethnicity, nationality or religion. Cultures themselves have become globalized and flow in unexpected ways around the world, interacting with and influencing each other, and a whole new vocabulary has emerged in attempts to describe and understand this—multiculturalism, hybridity, flows, transnationalism, cosmopolitanism, transborder, postmodernism, postcolonialism and even the "clash of civilizations". All of these are set in the context of the virtual hegemony of neo-liberal capitalism and the forms of consumer society that it generates, and with it the erosion of the power and significance of traditional nation-states. This in turn has challenged ideas of citizenship and raised interesting questions about whether new forms of "cosmopolitan citizenship" are appropriate, something encouraged by the emergence of new blocs with free movement and largely common currencies, such as the EU. Encouraging in many respects as such an idea is, it too needs to be handled critically, as there is always the danger that new "transnational spaces" may prove not to be so much genuinely cosmopolitan, as representing the cultural hegemony of certain politically and economically powerful actors, leading once again to the marginalization of those on the "edges" of the dominant world system, leading to the de facto diminution of real cultural diversity.

Culture cannot be "managed" and where such attempts at management appear, they are usually driven by political motives, sadly often ones of channeling or suppressing cultural expressions. For this reason, the parallel idea of "cultural policy" also needs to be handled with care, in situations when it does more than provide the facilities and possibly funding for cultural activities, without directly intervening in the creative process itself. Many successful examples of such enlightened policies do indeed exist, and even such bodies at UNESCO and the United Nations Development Program (UNDP) have started to recognize the importance of encouraging the "culture industries"—theatre, the visual arts, crafts, local filmmakers, music, dance and architecture—as significant contributors to development and to income generation, as well as for their intrinsic value (UNESCO/UNDP 2013). Such policies, to be effective, require both legal protections (again the issue of copyright and intellectual and creative property rights), and marketing, without which they remain invisible outside of their immediate local or regional context. Culture, then stands at the heart of holistic development, and cultural rights in turn are the mechanism for both protecting cultural expressions and allowing their flourishing and development. It is not surprising that today many apparently political struggles are about culture, since they are about identity. This fact foregrounds not only culture as an abstract concept, but real struggles for recognition, the right to expression and the right to be protected against cultural appropriation. Globalization is of course a double-edged sword. While on the one hand it makes available to us the riches and variety of the world's cultures—its foods, music, fashions, crafts, film and other cultural expressions—on the other it tends to radically homogenize and to drive to the edges those cultures which have not succeeded in achieving, or have not sought, visibility on the global stage. At the heart of globalization lay both an epistemological issue—the validity of many forms of knowledge and expression, and a justice issue—the rights of all cultures to recognition and fair evaluation in terms of what might be called a "polycentric aesthetics"—the equally valid range of cultural expressions that collectively make up the cultural diversity of the worldwide "culture sphere".

To summarize the key ideas to be explored in the following pages a multidimensional diagram might be imagined. This diagram represents the complex synergy between the elements in the "mix" that is being argued for here. This mix comprises a set of relationships: between culture and development, between human rights and development, between human rights and their expanded conception when understood as also including cultural rights, and the incorporation into development discourse of the essential factors of social justice and of sustainability. The master theme of the book is consequently the linking of development and cultural rights, the latter being a condensed or synthesizing concept that contains within itself the aspects of culture, of rights and of social justice, seen not only as the equitable distribution of economic benefits, but also as access to and the ability to express and expand specifically cultural capabilities and potentialities directed toward the creation of a humane and very livable and convivial worlds. One of its distinguishing features is the insertion into this rights discourse of issues of aesthetics, peace, narrative and the sociology of the body, factors which do not normally appear either in debates about rights (including, curiously, cultural ones), or about development. Their inclusion here is designed to greatly widen those discourses to include vital elements of culture without which both rights and development are left impoverished.

Seeking Cultural Rights

This book then, is not an attempt to provide a definitive and rigorous theory of cultural rights, but rather an exploration of where the pursuit of such rights might take us in conceiving of a more holistic conception of development, and how such a notion of cultural rights might be expanded to intersect with debates in what I see as parallel areas of concern, but which are rarely connected to the idea of cultural rights as an organizing concept. Centered on such a notion, the book will move through a range of questions which all circle back to the core question, and as such will attempt to open up some new "spaces" in which a kind of "alternative" thinking about culture and development can be attempted. The book is therefore more of an experiment than it is a final statement—it is in fact an exploration, one undertaken in the hope that by expanding ideas, new visions and strategies for achieving a sustainable future might come into view and into practice.

The substantive part of the book then begins with a detailed discussion of the concept of cultural rights, and how it is in turn related to development and to the major theme that has now emerged to frame these and other debates—notably sustainability. The role of that foundational chapter is not only to set out some fundamental parameters, but also to relate them to one another in a systematic way that creates a new synergy: out of newly defined relationships can come fresh paradigms. This Introduction has stressed the importance of seeing the issues of cultural rights and development as aspects of ethics. Chapter 3 takes up this issue specifically in the hope of refurbishing the importance of development ethics as a foundational part of development studies and of development practice, and relates this to the role of business, a major absence in many discussions of either rights or development except in the contexts in which business is identified with the (undoubted) evils of neo-liberal capitalism. Chapter 4 takes up the question of multiculturalism as the empirical situation in which most cultural discussion now takes place (whether or not the word itself is used), and argues in continuity with the preceding chapter that new issues of global ethics are implied by the coexistence of many interacting and sometimes competing cultures, as the new norm in a situation where isolated cultures or ones defined in essentialist terms, really no longer exist. This is to a large extent due to the processes of globalization and transnationalism at the basis of the hybridization of cultures that now defines the world situation, and Chapter 5 specifically addresses this situation and its implications.

The second part of the book considers a range of exemplars—case studies that illustrate the themes set out in the first part of the volume. These hopefully illuminate four examples, and also different approaches. Chapter 6 then examines the subject of art, clearly a major part of virtually all cultures, but which is rarely included within the ambit of development studies, and Chapter 7 the question of peace and considers the argument that there is a right to peace and relates this to both questions of culture and to the desire for holistic and non-violent forms of development. Chapter 8 introduces into the study of culture and development a very neglected, indeed almost invisible, dimension of concern—the body and the unexplored notion of the erotics of development. The third and final part of the book suggest two main themes—the important need to generate new stories—new narratives—to shape the emergence of future society on the one hand, and the nature of cultural activism needed to create and advance cultural rights on the other and the factors that inform, energize and underpin progressive and humane activism. Collectively the chapters that make up the book both offer an argument for the importance of the recognition of cultural rights as a part of an expanded conception of human rights, of the importance of protecting and advancing such rights as a vital contribution to the maintaining of the cultural diversity on which so much of the human future depends, and the essential link between both culture and cultural rights, and the creation of social justice and just and holistic development. Despite the controversies that surround this final word, no one can deny the reality of the profound problems of poverty, habitat destruction, pollution, conflict and resource depletion that characterize our contemporary historical situation, and the social inequalities and cruelties that they generate and which in so many cases sustain a deeply unequal world, despite our technological prowess and the accumulated experience of generations of interventions to encourage positive processes of social change. Can we seek a key to these failures in the nature of our culture, and possible solutions in a revitalized vision of culture as it might be and needs to be if we are to achieve not only a sustainable future in a minimalist sense, but an abundant future, not only or even in material terms, but in terms of cultural richness and satisfaction?

References

Anheier, Helmut, and Yudhishthir Raj Isar (eds.). 2011. *Heritage, Memory and Identity*. Los Angeles and London: Sage.

An-Naim, Abdullahi Ahmed. 1992. *Human Rights in Cross-Cultural Perspective*. Pittsburgh: University of Pennsylvania Press.

Bell, Lynda S., Andrew J. Nathan, and Ilan Peleg. 2001. *Negotiating Culture and Human Rights*. New York: Columbia University Press.
Bhabha, Homi K. 1994. *The Location of Culture*. London and New York: Routledge.
Bharucha, Rustom. 1993. *Theatre and the World: Performance and the Politics of Culture*. London and New York: Routledge.
Clammer, John. 1996. *Values and Development in Southeast Asia*. Petaling Jaya: Pelanduk.
Clammer, John. 2009. *Diaspora and Belief: Globalization, Religion and Identity in Postcolonial Asia*. New Delhi: Shipra Publications.
Clammer, John. 2012. *Culture, Development and Social Theory: Towards an Integrated Social Development*. London and New York: Zed Books.
Clammer, John. 2016. *Cultures of Transition and Sustainability*. New York and Basingstoke: Palgrave Macmillan.
Clammer, John, Sylvie Poirier, and Eric Schwimmer (eds.). 2004. *Figures Worlds: Ontological Obstacles in Intercultural Relations*. Toronto and London: Toronto University Press.
Cowan, Jane K., Marie-Benedict Dembour, and Richard A. Wilson (eds.). 2001. *Culture and Rights: Anthropological Perspectives*. Cambridge: Cambridge University Press.
Craven, Matthew C.R. 1995. *The International Convention on Economic, Social and Cultural Rights: A Perspective on Its Development*. Oxford: Clarendon Press.
De Beukelaer, Christiaan, Miikka Pyykkonen, and J.P. Singh (eds.). 2015. *Globalization, Culture and Development: The UNESCO Convention on Cultural Diversity*. Basingstoke and New York: Palgrave Macmillan.
Eide, Asbjorn, Catarina Krause, and Allan Rosas. 1995. *Economic, Social and Cultural Rights: A Textbook*. The Hague: Martinus Nijhoff Publishers.
Ghosh, Amitav. 2016. *The Great Derangement: Climate Change and the Unthinkable*. Gurgaon: Allen Lane India.
Gottlieb, Roger S. (ed.). 2004. *This Sacred Earth: Religion, Nature, Environment*, 2nd ed. New York and London: Routledge.
Gottlieb, Roger S. 2006. *A Greener Faith: Religious Environmentalism and Our Planet's Future*. New York and Oxford: Oxford University Press.
Hobsbawm, Eric. 2014. *Fractured Times: Culture and Society in the Twentieth Century*. London: Abacus.
Jacobsen, Michael, and Ole Bruun (eds.). 2003. *Human Rights and Asian Values: Contesting National Identities and Cultural Representations in Asia*. London: Curzon Press for the Nordic Institute of Asian Studies.
Klein, Naomi. 2015. *This Changes Everything*. London: Penguin Books.
Kleinman, Arthur, Veena Das, and Margaret Lock (eds.). 1997. *Social Suffering*. Berkeley and London: University of California Press.

Lewallen, Ann-Elise. 2016. *The Fabric of Indigeneity: Ainu Identity, Gender and Settler Colonialism in Japan*. Santa Fe: School for Advanced Research Press.
Maffesoli, Michel. 1996. *The Time of the Tribes: The Decline of Individualism in Mass Society*. London: Sage.
Nandy, Ashis. 1983. *The Intimate Enemy: Loss and Recovery of Self Under Colonialism*. New Delhi: Oxford University Press.
Nandy, Ashis. 1990. *At the Edge of Psychology: Essays in Politics and Culture*. New Delhi: Oxford University Press.
Nussbaum, Martha. 2011. *Creating Capabilities: The Human Development Approach*. Cambridge, MA: Belknap Press of Harvard University Press.
Nussbaum, Martha. 2012. *Not for Profit: Why Democracy Needs the Humanities*. Princeton and London: Princeton University Press.
Sachs, Wolfgang (ed.). 1995. *The Development Dictionary: A Guide to Knowledge*. London and New York: Zed Books.
Sen, Amartya. 2011. *The Idea of Justice*. Cambridge, MA: Belknap Press of Harvard University Press.
Thornberry, Patrick. 2002. *Indigenous Peoples and Human Rights*. Manchester: Manchester University Press.
UNESCO. 2005. *Convention on the Protection and Promotion of the Diversity of Cultural Expressions*. Paris: UNESCO.
UNESCO (United Nations Educational, Scientific and Cultural Organization) and UNDP (United Nations Development Program). 2013. *Creative Economy Report 2013: Widening Local Development Pathways*. Paris and New York: UNESCO and UNDP.
United Nations Office of the High Commissioner for Human Rights. 2005. *Economic, Social and Cultural Rights: A Handbook for National Human Rights Institutions*. Geneva: UN High Commission for Human Rights.
Urry, John. 2013. *Societies Beyond Oil: Oil Dregs and Social Futures*. London and New York: Zed Books.
Vickery, Jonathan. 2018. Arts Rights Justice: Protecting and Promoting Artistic Freedom: An Interview with Daniel Gad. *Journal of Law, Social Justice and Global Development* 22: 1–6.
Wilson, Richard A. (ed.). 1997. *Human Rights, Culture and Context: Anthropological Perspectives*. London: Pluto Press.
Young, Alison. 2005. *Judging the Image: Art, Value, Law*. London and New York: Routledge.

CHAPTER 2

Cultural Rights, Development and Sustainability

The linking of rights—particularly human rights—and development, is not a new idea. But a new configuration can be achieved by both expanding the range of human rights to include cultural rights, and in turn relating this to both development and to the newer lens through which many global problems are now being focused—notably sustainability. This chapter will explore this tripartite relationship and will insert that discussion into possible ways of reconceiving the broad interface of culture and development in more holistic ways than have generally been achieved.

The perceived failure of much "development" has had at least one salutary consequence—the recognition that the absence of the cultural dimension is at the root of many of these failures, and that, as a result, the reintroduction of a cultural perspective is a vital dimension of a holistic conception of development, and in particular defining more clearly what the goals of "development" should be (Schech and Haggis 2000; Radcliffe 2006; Clammer 2012). At the same time, the increasing recognition of the totally unsustainable nature of most existing patterns of development and its highly negative impact on the environment, has moved the notion of sustainability to a central place in contemporary discourses. Rights too—whether the right to development or the right to socially just forms of that process, however defined, have become a subject of debate and policy—in the latter case, for example, of whether

J. Clammer, *Cultural Rights and Justice*,
https://doi.org/10.1007/978-981-13-2811-4_2

to tie development aid to improvements in the human rights record of recipient countries. The question then arises of to what extent *cultural* rights, as an extension of the principles set out in the Universal Declaration of Human Rights should be or can be incorporated into discussions of sustainable development.

Within less than two decades after the promulgation of the Universal Declaration, some of its gaps and lacunae became to be recognized, resulting in 1966 of the adoption by the United Nations and its constituent states of two additional treaties—the International Covenant on Civil and Political Rights (ICCPR), and the International Covenant on Economic, Social and Cultural Rights (ICESCR). Although the latter does contain the word "culture" in its title, it does not actually define cultural rights or indicate which of its provisions specifically relate to the protection of cultural rights. The relationship between human rights and cultural rights is consequently left vague in these major international legal instruments. Yvonne Donders has attempted to clarify this confusion by proposing a definition of cultural rights and their scope: "Cultural rights can be broadly defined as human rights that directly promote and protect cultural interests of individuals and communities and that are meant to advance their capacity to preserve, develop and change their cultural identity" (Donders 2015: 117). She expands this minimal definition by arguing that such rights not only include those that specifically mention culture, but also those broader human rights that have a direct link to cultural freedom, such as the rights to self-determination, to education, to free expression and freedom of religion, and to those principles embodied in such international instruments as UNESCO's 2001 Universal Declaration on Cultural Diversity in which cultural rights are regarded as necessary for the expression of that cultural diversity. From this perspective, cultural rights can be identified as a subsection or extension of "general" human rights. In one way of course it is strange to need to speak about culture as a "right" at all, since everyone has a culture. But the key issue is not the "possession" of a culture, but rather the tragic fact that in so many cases cultural rights are threatened by censorship, suppression, erosion, exclusion or displacement. There are indeed many cases in which the possibility of the expression or preservation of culture is extremely difficult, as in Balfour (2013).

Culture and Development Revisited

The renewed movement toward more systematically relating culture and development has taken a number of forms, including the pragmatic argument that culture contributes to the "delivery" of development goods. Examples indeed abound of the necessity of taking culture into account in many contexts such as health provision, where local ideas of the body, gender, disease causation, witchcraft and magic may have a significant impact on the successful implementation of well-meaning, but culturally inappropriate health care plans (Samson 2004). Similarly, in agriculture including the adoption of crops that are new to indigenous diets, housing and architecture—for example, in post-disaster reconstruction (Aquilino 2011), and in many other situations (for a rather dated but still excellent set of case studies see Dove 1980). In such cases culture has a primarily instrumental role, but such a limited viewpoint has been expanded in some fruitful ways, for example, by the encouragement by UN agencies such as UNESCO and the UN Development Program (UNDP) of "creative industries"—drawing on indigenous cultural production (music, performance, crafts and visual arts) as an important and neglected economic resource for income generation in "developing" communities, and indeed, as a source of self-respect, empowerment and dignity (UNESCO/UNCTAD 2008; Kabanda 2014). This approach has interesting affinities with the older "human needs" approach, in which in virtually every list aesthetic needs and the needs for expression and leisure are prominent (Dube 1984). This is expanded even further in recent discussion of the role of the arts in development which not only argue for the utility of the arts in income generation, but also for their essential role in actually constituting culture and their important role in establishing dignity, identity, imagination and creativity (Clammer 2015). All of which points to a holistic conception of development in pursuing both its means and its ends.

The question then arises of the relationship of sustainability to both cultural rights and development. There are at least three dimensions of this relationship that can be identified. The first is the relationship between cultural diversity and biodiversity. Local notions of ecology are embodied in indigenous languages and cultural practices, and with the loss or erosion of such local knowledge many sustainable practices are also lost and are largely impossible to recover. Secondly, while biologists recognize that biodiversity strengthens the entire biosphere and that the loss of one seemingly insignificant species (the bee or the bat, which both play major roles as pollinators for example), it is not unreasonable to extend the same line of reasoning to human cultures. The loss of cultural diversity diminishes the whole as knowledge, alternative lifestyles, long sustained relationships with the environment and particular species within it, forms of music, performance, cuisines, languages, technologies, cosmologies and kinship possibilities are lost forever. The preamble to the UNESCO 2005 Convention on the Protection and Promotion of the Diversity of Cultural Expressions immediately recognizes this and for "the need to take measures to protect the diversity of cultural expressions, including their contents, especially in situations where cultural expressions may be threatened by the possibility of extinction or serious impairment".

The third dimension relates to the consequences of the emergence, in the affluent societies and among the rising middle classes of the developing ones, of consumption cultures that are inherently unsustainable—its extractive economy, buy-and-throw-away attitude, excessive use of non-renewable energy resources, polluting character and so on. This should alert us to the intimate connections between culture and economy, an economy which, despite its posturing to the contrary, actually constrains our choices and deeply shapes our subjectivities while causing irreversible damage to the environment on which we all depend. Sustainability and culture are inseparably connected: it is precisely our "civilization" that has brought about most of the elements in the planetary crisis that we now collectively confront, and so it is only by changing the destructive cultural patterns that have generated the crisis, that a truly sustainable future can be envisaged.

The recognition of this implies a number of steps, of which the first is the expansion of the category of human rights to include cultural rights, and to ensure that such rights are not subordinated to others found in the original UDHR. Rights alone, at least on paper, do not guarantee their observance or translation into practice. To do this means the cultivation of cultural practices that are both sustainable and just, a cultivation that also means considering the rights of nature and of other species. Such a culture would also link the idea of rights to that of responsibilities, since a culture of purely entitlements is likely to be destructive of both the rights and liberties of others, and of the environment. The notion of social justice should then include cultural justice, with the latter containing some perhaps unexpected elements such as what I have elsewhere and in Chapter 6 called "visual justice"—the right to beauty and an aesthetically pleasing environment and a reduction in the ugliness and bad design that so often accompanies "development", city planning and contemporary architecture (Clammer 2014; Schwartz and Krabbendam 2013). All this requires cultural activism as much as the political variety, or, indeed, to merge the two into new forms of socially transformative movements.

Interrogating Cultural Rights

The argument so far has been that cultural rights are closely connected to both development and sustainability through many intimate links, including sustainable cultural practices in consumption patterns, transport choices, urban planning, and very much so in relation to the arts, architecture and design (Kagan 2011). Cultures are both expressions of and sources of imagination, including what we might call "social imagination"—ideas that promote new and hopefully positive and sustainable patterns of social change and transformation. The development *of* culture is in a very real sense "development"—the creation of spaces of meaning and freedom beyond politics and economics in their narrow sense, the source of alternatives, the watering of the roots of identity, and the generator of the cultural and aesthetic pluralism that constitutes the diversity that parallels in significance the biodiversity on which the web of life depends. A number of approaches can be taken to this, whether anthropological ones, or through the development of international legal instruments such as those emerging from UNESCO, the one UN body specifically charged with overseeing culture, of which the most recent major one is the 2005 *Convention on the Protection and Promotion of Cultural Diversity* (UNESCO 2005).

The ways in which this document both conceptualizes culture and understands its relationship to development is both significant and contestable. The preamble to the Convention, while never attempting to define its operative concept of culture, sets out, in typical UN-speak, a series of propositions. Having stated that it regards cultural diversity as a normal characteristic of humanity and that it is a global common heritage and should be cherished, the Convention develops these propositions: "*Being aware* that cultural diversity creates a rich and varied world, which increase the range of choices and nurtures human capacities and values, and therefore is a mainspring for sustainable development for communities, peoples and nations", *Recalling* that cultural diversity flourishing within a framework of democracy, tolerance, social justice and mutual respect between peoples and cultures, is indispensable for peace and security at the local, national and international levels", and *Celebrating* the importance of cultural diversity for the full realization of human rights and fundamental freedoms proclaimed in the Universal Declaration of Human Rights and other universally recognized instruments". Having set out these claims, the Convention goes on to argue, without any concrete suggestions of how to do so, for the need to incorporate culture into national and international development policies, and to protect cultures from erosion, especially under the impact of globalization. The subsequent Articles reaffirm the importance of the link between culture and development, and specifically asserts in Article 2, subsection ("Principles of Sustainable Development") that "The protection, promotion and maintenance of cultural diversity are essential requirements for sustainable development for the benefit of present and future generations", and again repeats itself in Article 13: "Parties shall endeavor to integrate culture in their development policies at all levels for the creation of conditions conducive to sustainable development, and, within this framework, foster aspects relating to the protection and promotion of cultural expressions". The Convention suggests a number of ways in which this might be done, including strengthening cultural industries, allowing fair access to global markets for developing country cultural products, cultural capacity building, and the promotion of the mobility of artists from the developing world. Very woolly in its language, without sanctions or concrete methods for achieving its goals—left specifically up the goodwill of signatory governments—and without actually defining the concept of cultural rights, the Convention is clearly a well-meaning but ineffective instruments for promoting those rights and the broader field of social justice which they are supposed to embody. But this weakness points to where the lacunae exist, and by filling them in, to more fully defining the links between culture and development.

A significant dimension of the Covenant is that it specifically relates cultural rights to human rights, and culture to sustainability. Whether the logic that links these in the Convention is very clear is another question, but at least this triangulation has been put on the table for debate. To "operationalize" it a number of steps would have to be made. The first of these is to recognize that all people "have" a culture, and that all cultures are in principle equal. The question of equality arises in relation to such issues as female genital mutilation or, historically, cannibalism, and today to non-sustainable cultural practices such as excessive waste generation. Cultures themselves evolve over time. As Foucault and others have documented, in Western cultures disciplinary regimes have evolved from the brutality of violent and bloody public executions toward much more psychologically based forms, and from the infliction of pain on the body toward rehabilitative work on the "soul". The principle of equality also points to the dissolution of any distinction between "high" and "popular" cultures, since we know that in practice these draw on each other, "quote" each other, and interact in numerous ways (in advertising for example). Many forms of "craft" are, in terms of workmanship and aesthetic qualities, often far superior to many manifestations of contemporary art, and many forms of performance art are rooted in ritual, religious practices or ecological and agricultural practices that are an integral part of a local culture, and not put on for purely entertainment purposes.

While an instrumental approach to culture and development, whether as seeking culturally appropriate ways of conceiving of or delivery, or as the encouragement of cultural industries, is important, it should not obscure the fact that culture runs much deeper. It represents worldviews, forms of expression and meaning generation (often embodied in religion), aesthetics, and the ways in which the latter is manifested in verbal, visual, architectural and performative forms. It is also intrinsically holistic in that it encompasses such themes rarely discussed in the development literature such as food, costume, bodily decoration, music, hair, sexuality, sport and design, and intersects in fundamental ways with economy, kinship and indigenous legal conceptions and practices. The notion of the development *of* culture recognizes that culture is not an abstract idea, but a set of concrete manifestations, and the active encouragement and strengthening of these is real development, and reflects in a very practical way the "capabilities" approach promoted by such scholars as Amartya Sen (2009) and Martha Nussbaum (2011). This constitutes cultural rights at work. It suggests too a conception of development which is based on a strong form of social justice—one in which there is also freedom of expression and the creation of a situation in which cultural rights can be exercised, and on a vision of an abundant life in which creative cultural expression is an organic part of everyday life. One could certainly argue that the poverty of many development policies and practices is that they solely generate an image of life dominated by the economic, rather than to a picture in which creativity and imagination are given full play. This is certainly reflected in the fact that few aid agencies fund cultural work, and that when governments decide that they need to cut budgets, the first thing to go is usually funding for the arts and for such essential cultural institutions as libraries and museums.

Martha Nussbaum and others have cogently argued that cultural development and its expression in the humanities and in liberal education, is essential to the creation and sustaining of democracy (Nussbaum 2012). The notion of cultural rights may then be extended to encompass not only the protection of existing forms of cultural diversity, but also the right to be exposed to such forms through entitlement to a humanistic education and the incorporation of this into technical, managerial and legal education. Imagination and creativity need not be confined to the arts alone, but spill over into any number of other fields, providing the tools to rethink such socially fundamental categories as gender, ethnicity or sexual and subcultural differences. It also allows local conceptions of "heritage" to be embraced, and, as UNESCO itself has done, to extend this notion from purely material remains to what it is calling "intangible culture heritage", a category including folklore, oral traditions and stories, local musical forms, folk dances and many other "popular" but non-material expressions of culture. It also allows the expansion of what sociologists in particular consider to be social movements, it being evident that many cultural movements are also examples of social movements, whether, say, Surrealism in the West of the 1920s–1930s, or the Mayan Rights movement in central America, in which rights are seen not only as political and economic, but also very much as cultural, and in which the struggle for cultural rights is part of a holistic conception of identity and development (Davis 2004).

Cultural Rights, Multiculturalism and the Cosmopolitan

An essentialist definition of culture tends toward the static, but stasis can hardly be taken to be the condition of culture in the contemporary world. Here we can not only invoke globalization, but also seemingly non-cultural processes such as climate change, which in fact have profound effects on cultural practices and conceptions of the world in which such practices might flourish—or not. A static view of culture is what, in critiquing the work of the anthropologist Jonathan Friedman (1999), Nikos Papastergiadis calls a "residentialist" conception of culture—notably one that denies hybridity and mobility and which assumes that "Symbolic practices were supposedly confined to the physical and territorial boundaries of a given place" (Papastergiadis 2012: 125), and which has the corollary that someone uprooted from or disconnected from the original place of belonging is "severed from the cultural system that holds together the whole set of identifications". Such a view of culture, which is very close to the one embodied in the UNESCO Convention, makes at least three important and contestable assumptions: that cultures are spatially rooted (presumably in only one place), that identity is tied to such a specific location (in effect a kind of cultural nationalism) such that mobility destroys that vital connection, and that consequently hybrid cultures are inauthentic, so a cosmopolitan subjectivity means rootlessness. These assumptions can be contested both theoretically and empirically, and need to be since they have significant consequences for both the notions of cultural rights and of cultural diversity. The UNESCO understanding of culture does appear to be highly "residentialist" in assuming that culture exists in particular spaces, but not between them. This is why they need to be "protected" from globalization. It seems hardly necessary to even argue against this view: it is glaringly obvious that cultures, like people, "travel", that they constantly recompose themselves in dialogue, conflict or merger, and that there are no "pure" cultures since hybridity is now the norm rather than the exception. There is plenty of evidence that migrants successfully reconstitute a variety of their original culture in ways that interface with the new host culture—modifying habits of food, dress, body language, housing and so forth, while retaining religious identity and many aspects of kinship and marriage customs. It is also evident that many such persons do not feel any problem about their "identity" (itself a very imprecise concept), but successfully formulate new subjectivities appropriate to and quite comfortable with, their new spatial and cultural situation.

The notion of cultural rights then cannot be tied to a static conception of culture, since such cultures rarely exist. On the contrary, it must be argued that the notion of rights needs to be recast in "hybrid" terms. This does not dissolve the idea that cultural rights can indeed refer to the preservation and the right to practice an "original" culture (however that is conceived or constructed), but expands it to allow for the rights of hybrid cultural forms to be equally respected. The political dimension is of this is clear: claim for the special protection of (only) "original" rights often mask at best a form of nationalism and at worst barely disguised forms of fundamentalism. Opposed to this are voice suggesting that what is emerging on a global scale is a new form of cosmopolitanism, fed by the internet and reflecting new ways of "belonging" or asserting and creating identity (Creed 2003), or taking the position of Paul Gilroy that what we are seeing is a new "planetary humanism" emerging from and fed new forms of urban conviviality and transnational human rights movements (Gilroy 2004: 28). Certainly these are optimistic voices, but they do point to the real possibility of new forms of cosmopolitan identity, no longer necessarily rooted either in a particular place or the spaces in between, but in a new form of space constituted out of the processes of globalization and cultural transnationalism. This also suggests that universals can exist at some levels (e.g. the ideals of the UDHR), while diversity can be celebrated at others, whether in local cultures or in the hybrid forms that cultural pluralism typically takes. New forms of "cultural translation" are then required as mediation between cultural forms take place and as interpretation is constantly needed between what used to be called nations, between generations, between generations, between one culture of origin and others, and between any one culture of origins and its own emerging transformations.

There are many points of contact between debates about the possibility and nature of cosmopolitan identities and debates about multiculturalism, although the two should not be confused (a subject that will be taken up in subsequent chapters). Multiculturalism suggests a situation in which a number of cultures coexist together, without achieving any substantial degree of integration, while cosmopolitanism suggests either a melding of cultural identities or a transcending of cultural differences in favor of more universalized sense of identity. But even the concept of multiculturalism undermines any essentialist or "residentialist" notions of culture, or at the very least, posits the spatial and temporal coexistence of multiple residential cultures (if such exist), perhaps aware of each other's existence, although not necessarily interacting with one another. For Kant, for whom the development of appropriate political formations was a prerequisite for cultural rights to emerge, it follows that, as Papastergiadis puts it "Cosmopolitanism is not a virtue that is to be pursued for its own qualities, but is dependent on the developments within a political process that seeks to control the destructive drives in human nature, as well as to temper the tyrannical abuses of power" (Papastergiadis 2012: 83). The simple diversity of cultures does not guarantee that all are benign, committed to the integrity or autonomy of other cultures, or environmentally responsible. Far from it: as history all to bleakly demonstrates, some cultures whatever their cultural "level", may be predatory, colonialist or assimilative of others in the total cultural ecology. This suggests the role of power in cultural relationships: all cultures may be born equal, but they do not necessarily remain so in practice.

So while what Papastergiadis calls a "cosmopolitan imagery" is certainly a goal to pursue (unless one is a hard-core residentialist), its very possibility assumes its incorporation into a complex understanding of hybridity. We see many elements of this at work around us: the incorporation of "foreign" material into the construction of identities and the process of assimilation or attempted neutralization of such elements, individual and communal strategies of openness to new influences while still retaining attachment to other dimensions of identity such as the religion of one's birth. The nature of the public sphere is correspondingly transformed and becomes a culturally fluid space in which all the actors concerned are, if not transformed, certainly influenced by the process of "culture contact" with which they are necessarily involved. This can lead to new group formation, or, crucially, to new forms of social exclusion (Nederveen Pieterse 2001). Cultural rights, then, have not only to recognize the dynamic nature of culture, but also to grasp that cultural interaction is not equal, but an aspect of power relations. "Diversity" in itself tells us nothing about the actual domination of some cultures and the marginalization of others in the total global cultural ecology. Cosmopolitan cultures have always existed, and the collaborative methodologies now widely employed among artists, scientists, ethnic groups and coreligionists are witness to this process. Without recognition of culture as a primary site of struggle, the notion of cultural rights is largely unnecessary. It is precisely because culture is such a contested zone, and one linked intimately with politics, that the salience of cultural rights emerges.

Development, Culture and Social Justice

Development is a highly plural project, one that necessarily includes culture, and, if to last, must sustainable. Cultural policies as a result enter development discourse every bit as much as do economic ones. Authentic development must be rooted in the soils of local cultures or it withers, and the many development failures that litter the social landscape are testimony to this, as the anthropologist James Scott and others have so pointedly documented (Scott 1998). This is, in many cases, the result of the failure to adequately triangulate culture, development and sustainability. Some of the elements in this triangulation have already been indicated—the fostering of "ecological cultures" as a basis for sustainable development; the rethinking of concepts of citizenship, multiculturalism and cosmopolitanism in the context of a shared and globalized world, a rethinking tied again to the question of the environment and the emergence of an "ecological citizenship" (Davidson 2004); and a global ethics—one of mutual responsibility rather than an individualistic one or one rooted in purely local or political considerations. The very word "cosmopolitan" means to be linked to a larger whole. Some scholars of multiculturalism have suggested that the kind of cultural diversity embodied in the UNESCO document represents a form of "liberal multiculturalism" (Kymlicka 2005)—a well-meaning but hardly proactive concept that does not uncover the full implications of an authentic multiculturalism, a notion that would include a culturally multipolar world and one in which globalization, rather than homogenizing cultures supports genuine difference and the existence of many alternative epistemologies and cultural ontologies. Culture is not only what is, but also what might be, the very existence of literary fiction being exactly the means of creating alternative visions, as the eminent novelist Mario Vargas Llosa has so cogently argued (Llosa 2007).

This discussion points to a number of propositions which can be summarized as follows:

1. That cultural rights, sustainability and development form a triangle of necessarily related elements.
2. That cultural rights are an integral part of human rights, and both are related to the rights of nature.
3. Critiques of the supposed universalism of human rights as they are embodied in the UDHR have largely taken the form of arguing

that there are cultural variations that mean that human rights should be contextualized in relation to particular cultures. Leaving aside the self-serving motives of some governments that have asserted this position in order to dilute their commitment to the protection of certain rights, the incorporation of cultural rights as an aspect of human rights goes a long way to meeting this objection.

4. Cultural rights must recognize the autonomy of particular aesthetic expressions, a recognition that gives cultural rights a critical edge by not simply acknowledging diversity (a patronizing position), but recognizing them as genuine alternatives and equally viable epistemologies and ontologies—of ways of seeing the world and being in that world. No culture can claim a monopoly as having *the* correct worldview. There is no such thing.
5. All cultures evolve and change, but should, except when clear violation of fundamental human rights occur behind the smokescreen of claims to cultural exceptionalism, be allowed to evolve at their own pace. The alternative is a kind of cultural colonialism in which the more economically and politically powerful societies seek to impose their own cultures on the rest of the world, often today in the name of "soft power", but leading to forms of cultural homogeneity quite at variance with the goal of the protection and promotion of cultural diversity.
6. Given the imbalances in power, politically, economically, technologically and culturally in the contemporary world—imbalances enhanced rather than diminished by globalization—pro-active cultural policies should seek not only to protect, but also to actively support indigenous cultures in all their variety, to encourage cultural experimentation and new forms of art. Aid agencies should see it as part of their duty to support culture as an essential part of holistic development.

We are in a situation in which development fails without culture, as does any realistic notion of sustainability, and it is now much more widely recognized that culture is a "pillar of sustainability" (Hawkes 2001). The bottom line then is an expanded notion of human rights that not only includes cultural rights, but which sees the fulfillment or achievement of a rights-based world as constituting the nature of sustainability and the purpose or end of development. Social justice is the non-negotiable project, but with the recognition that social justice must include both cultural and ecological justice in the conceptualization of development as a holistic and life-enhancing process.

References

Aquilino, Marie J. (ed.). 2011. *Beyond Shelter: Architecture of Crisis*. London: Thames and Hudson.

Balfour, Michael (ed.). 2013. *Refugee Performance: Practical Encounters*. Bristol and Chicago: Intellect.

Clammer, John. 2012. *Culture, Development and Social Theory: Towards an Integrated Social Development*. London and New York: Zed Books.

Clammer, John. 2014. *Vision and Society: Towards a Sociology and Anthropology from Art*. Abingdon and New York: Routledge.

Clammer, John. 2015. *Art, Culture and International Development: Humanizing Social Transformation*. Abingdon and New York: Routledge.

Creed, B. 2003. *Media Matrix: Sexing the New Reality*. Crows Nest, NSW: Allen and Unwin.

Davidson, Julie. 2004. Citizenship and Sustainability: Rights and Responsibilities in the Global Age. In *Controversies in Environmental Sociology*, ed. Rob White, 168–184. Cambridge: Cambridge University Press.

Davis, S.H. 2004. The Mayan Movement and National Culture in Guatemala. In *Culture and Public Action: A Cross-Disciplinary Dialogue on Development Policy*, ed. V. Rao and M. Walton. Stanford: Stanford University Press.

Donders, Yvonne. 2015. Cultural Human Rights and the UNESCO Convention: More Than Meets the Eye? In *Globalization, Culture and Development: The UNESCO Convention on Cultural Diversity*, ed. Christiaan De Beukelaer, Miikka Pyykkonen, and J.P. Singh, 117–131. Basingstoke and New York: Palgrave Macmillan.

Dove, Michael (ed.). 1980. *The Real and Imagined Role of Culture in Development*. Honolulu: University of Hawai'i Press.

Dube, S.C. 1984. *Development Perspectives for the 1980s*. Kuala Lumpur: Pelanduk Publications for the United Nations Asian and Pacific Development Centre.

Friedman, Jonathan. 1999. The Hybridization of Roots and the Abhorrence of the Bush. In *Spaces of Culture: City, Nation, World*, ed. Mike Featherstone and Scott Lash, 230–256. London: Sage.

Gilroy, Paul. 2004. *After Empire: Melancholia or Convivial Culture?* London and New York: Routledge.

Hawkes, J. 2001. *The Fourth Pillar of Sustainability: Culture's Essential Role in Public Planning*. New York: Common Ground.

Kabanda, Patrick. 2014. *The Creative Wealth of Nations: How the Performing Arts Can Advance Development and Human Progress*. Washington, DC: World Bank Group.

Kagan, Sacha. 2011. *Art and Sustainability: Connecting Patterns for a Culture of Complexity*. Bielefeld: Transcript Verlag.

Kymlicka, W. 2005. Liberal Multiculturalism: Western Models, Global Trends and Asian Debates. In *Multiculturalism in Asia*, ed. W. Kymlicka and B. He, 22–55. Oxford: Oxford University Press.

Llosa, Mario Vargas. 2007. *Touchstones: Essays on Literature, Art and Politics*. Selected, trans. and ed. John King. London: Faber and Faber.

Nederveen Pieterse, Jan. 2001. Hybridity, So What? The Anti-hybridity Backlash and the Riddles of Recognition. *Theory, Culture and Society* 18 (2/3): 219–245.

Nussbaum, Martha. 2011. *Creating Capabilities: The Human Development Approach*. Cambridge, MA: Belknap Press of Harvard University Press.

Nussbaum, Martha. 2012. *Not for Profit: Why Democracy Need the Humanities*. Princeton and London: Princeton University Press.

Papastergiadis, Nikos. 2012. *Cosmopolitanism and Culture*. Cambridge and Malden, MA: Polity Press.

Radcliffe, Sarah A. 2006. *Culture and Development in a Globalizing World: Geographies, Actors and Paradigms*. Abingdon and New York: Routledge.

Samson, Colin. 2004. We Live This Experience: Ontological Insecurity and Colonial Domination of the Innu People of Northern Labrador. In *Figured Worlds: Ontological Obstacles to Intercultural Relations*, ed. John Clammer, Sylvie Poirier, and Eric Schwimmer, 151–188. Toronto and London: Toronto University Press.

Schech, Susanne, and Jane Haggis. 2000. *Culture and Development: A Critical Introduction*. Oxford and Malden, MA: Blackwell.

Schwartz, Michel, and Diane Krabbendam. 2013. *Sustainist Design Guide*. Amsterdam: BIS Publishers.

Scott, James. 1998. *Seeing Like a State: How Certain Schemes to Improve the Human Condition Have Failed*. New Haven: Yale University Press.

Sen, Amartya. 2009. *The Idea of Justice*. Cambridge, MA: Belknap Press.

UNESCO (United Nations Educational, Scientific and Cultural Organization). 2005. *Convention on the Protection and Promotion of the Diversity of Cultural Expressions*. Paris: UNESCO.

UNESCO/UNCTAD. 2008. *Creative Economy*. Paris and Geneva: UNESCO and UNCTAD.

CHAPTER 3

Cultural Rights, Business and the Ethics of Development: Bringing Social Ethics Back In

Two things at least should be evident about the contemporary world. The first is that we face a global crisis of unprecedented proportions. Global warming and its associated climate change will have vast and as yet unknown effects on agriculture, rainfall patterns, temperatures, extreme weather and rising sea levels which will have huge impacts on the livelihoods or even survival of many millions. At the same time we see extensive pollution of the atmosphere, water and soils, unabated extraction of non-renewable resources, loss of biodiversity, extensive corruption within many societies, conflict and crime within and between societies, and new forms of crime emerging in tune with what were supposed to be benign technologies (cybercrime for example). The tragic and depressing list goes on—hyper-urbanization with its associated crowding and lack of facilities, soil loss, human trafficking, widening economic inequalities within and between nations, arms trading, terrorism, lack of access to educational or medical facilities on the part of many, persisting gender inequalities, child labor and no doubt even more examples that any of us could add. What is particularly frightening is that today, unlike periods in the past when some of these features were present, they are now all occurring together, and in a political environment that sees an international move to the Right (signaling less positive environmental legislation, unfriendliness to migrants, rolling back of social protections) and the election of "leaders" who seem to care little about these issues or are not willing to take unpopular but necessary steps to address them.

J. Clammer, *Cultural Rights and Justice*,
https://doi.org/10.1007/978-981-13-2811-4_3

The second is that, of all the social actors responsible, business, and in particular large corporations, are among the most responsible agents. It might indeed be argued that of all social actors, business is now the major one on a global scale. Yet the role of business in development discourse is often ignored, or simply banished to the category of "neo-liberal economics" and its pernicious effects on the world and attempts to create a holistic model of development. Politicians are often in thrall to business interests and it has been cogently argued that a great deal of so-called "political" policy is in fact just economics by another name, or to put it slightly differently, that it is economics (and not, e.g. environmental concerns or issues of social justice) that drive public policy, both domestically and internationally. Business is then in an ambiguous position as regards the sad list of problems enumerated above. On the one hand it can benefit (weak pollution controls, corruption in the granting of mining licenses, the favoring of certain kinds of migration policies over others, access to cheap and unregulated and un-unionized labor, the legal ability to keep people on short-term or even "Zero Hours" contracts and to be supported by the courts in doing so). On the other, because of its sheer size and power as a social actor, it can potentially address those problems that are within its zone of competence. Yet despite this, business rarely appears as an actor in development studies debates, and most textbooks in the field are innocent of any discussion of this major actor, one which, along with the world's militaries, has more impact on the environment and climate than most others put together. This is odd, not only because of its significance, but because other non-state actors (NGOs, international and multilateral organizations, social movements) do indeed appear prominently in the vocabulary of development studies. Furthermore, in the context of our discussion of culture, we forget how much of that culture is not only shaped, but directly created by business—all of the consumer products that we buy and utilize, almost all our entertainment, the shape of our holidays and the means of getting to our destinations, our possible fashion choices, the music available for us to listen to, the style of houses and their furnishings, and in many more respects. Discussion of business usually appears indirectly—as discussion and critique of globalization, and/or as a comment on the pernicious effects of neo-liberal capitalism. Given its significance, however defined, it clearly relates in absolutely central ways to development, to culture, potentially to the denial of cultural rights, and hence to ethics: the "right" of private, profit-driven entities, to act with relative impunity, in ecological, social and cultural spheres, toward which they may exercise little or no responsibility.

But in saying this it is important to distinguish direct from indirect effects. A responsible company may (and many do) aim to cut CO_2 emissions and other pollutants, not to foul rivers or other bodies of water and not to draw off groundwater needed by local farmers and other members of the surrounding communities. It can pay fair wages, have equitable gender policies, provide child care rather than exploit child labor, provide pensions and otherwise act in a highly positive way as almost, in the case of large companies in particular, as a kind of ministate pursuing very socially beneficial policies. But it may do none or few of these things. So while terrorism can hardly be traced to the activities of any legitimate business organization (illegitimate ones and those engaged in such activities as arms manufacture and trading are another issue), the long-term and hidden effects may indeed be there: destruction of the local economy and its traditional occupations, creating not unemployment but generating only low skilled monotonous jobs, the hollowing—out of communities as mega-malls and giant hypermarkets get constructed near small towns where modest local businesses were the mainstay, and illegally dumping toxic wastes in pristine environments, polluting the air and contributing to climate change.

Many of the critics of globalization make exactly these points: that the global economic playing field is not level, that there are losers as well as winners and that the multilateral financial and trade organizations (the World Bank, the IMF, and the WTO) are biased in the direction of supporting those who already have economic power. The history of globalization has been replete with examples of the destruction of local economies, displacement and marginalization of peoples, cultural erosion, the export of waste and polluting industries to the poorer countries, and the many other well-documented accounts of the "underside" of globalization, a process from which some have benefitted and many have suffered. The shining new cities of the Gulf States and Singapore have been quite literally built by temporary migrant labor (usually forbidden to settle in the places they have constructed) from India, Nepal, Bangladesh, Thailand and Indonesia. Virtually every middle-class Singapore family is served by a Filipina maid, who is often a college graduate and who may be better educated than her employers, but who cannot stay beyond the end of her contract and is forbidden to marry a local person. The disruption of family life that such sojourns abroad entail, justified only by the economic benefits of being able to remit money home, is considerable. But all these social processes are driven by what are indeed economic interests—the need for cheap, docile and expendable labor, or for a maid who will allow others to pursue active economically beneficial (to themselves) careers without problems of childcare or homework. In all these senses Karl Marx was basically correct: the economy underlies and to a great extent determines other levels of social reality—what we can earn, where we can live, our patterns of consumption, travel and movement, our status and our very subjectivities—our values in other words and our sense of self and hence of others.

Ethics, Business, Development and Responsibility

It should be quite clear that there is a close connection between the state of the world (which we have not found but created in its social, economic and political dimensions) and ethics. In a fairly obvious sense, business and management have an ethical dimension—not to cheat your customers, or to provide substandard products. To charge fair prices, to pay your suppliers on time. To be responsible for the "afterlife" of your products when they have reached the end of their reasonable utility. But given the context in which business must now operate, and equally given that this context is a planetary one today, the notion of business ethics must also be expanded beyond this limited range. It too must be a planetary ethics. Some of these principles are already embodied in widely accepted practices—the whole Fair Trade movement and the issues that motivate it (paying fair prices to primary producers of commodities such as coffee, handicrafts and handloom products, and assisting those producers to work in a sustainable and ecologically appropriate way), in international declarations such as the foundational Universal Declaration of Human Rights (not often cited however in business circles), and in emerging aspects of international law such as the law of the sea, laws pertaining to the exploitation of Antarctica, and the rise of environmental law as a whole new specialism. But these need filling out to relate them to the actual areas of concern that are the subject of this book, and this I will now attempt to do.

1. Resources. It is very obvious that we live in world of finite resources. Oil, coal, water, forests, even soil, are not unlimited. Yet resource extracting industries often act as if they were, and become

predatory in their search for new sources. A finite resource by definition cannot last forever; only renewable ones can. This simple fact has extensive ethical as well as practical implications. The practical ones, although rarely thought through in any detail except perhaps by the "Transition" movement (Hopkins 2008) and a number of scholars who have seriously addressed the questions of a post-oil society (Urry 2013) are actually immense. If we accept the argument of the Transition people that we have already passed the point of "peak oil"—the point at which economically recoverable sources have diminished to the extent that we are now entering a process of "energy decline" in which oil will become a rarer and hence more expensive commodity and that all the myriad processes and products on which our oil-based civilization depends will be harder and then eventually impossible to sustain—our modes of transport, heating and cooling, plastics and millions of products—and that consequently huge economic and social shifts will follow. The current "technological fixes"—moving to nuclear energy from oil or coal-based generation, or the extraction of oil from tar sands, which uses more energy than it produces (and vast quantities of water) and creates massive environmental damage—are all fraught with large (and in the case of nuclear waste, unresolvable) problems. Yet there is little systematic thought about either how to manage the enormous transition from an oil-based to an "alternative" form of society and economy, or of how we should plan rationally now for a future of little oil, an inevitability that has vast social and cultural implications as well as economic and technological ones.

The other aspect is of course ethical. What right do we have to quite literally burn non-renewable resources not only causing immense pollution, but depriving future generations of the benefits of access to the energy and products that are dependent on them? This raises significant philosophical questions—do we have responsibilities to future and as yet unborn generations? Do animals, and even plants, have rights? They inhabit the same biosphere as humans, and we are dependent on many of them for food, medicines, company and aesthetic pleasure. But is their relationship to us purely functional (i.e. we can exploit them as we like for our own human benefit without regard to their intrinsic interests?) Of course, longer-term thinking makes us realize that we *are* dependent on them, and cannot survive without them. Even an ethics of caution, regardless of extending this to the issue of the intrinsic rights of other species which we now treat simply as resources, would suggest that care of the natural environment is very much in human interests. (There is now a large and growing literature on the subject of environmental ethics. For a good survey, see Curry 2011.)

2. Climate Change. Here many of the same ethical issues apply. If indeed, as all the scientific evidence suggests, climate change is largely human-driven and created by aspects of "advanced" contemporary civilizations—primarily industrialization, but with it our addiction to the car, deforestation, meat-eating, unnecessary long-distance transportation by truck, sea or air of non-local commodities, extensive use of highly polluting energy generation methods (in particular coal) and the huge carbon footprints of our mega-cities with their traffic, trash generation, air-conditioning, commuting, and endless construction activities—then those societies are responsible. What is humanly created can be humanly modified, but therein lies the rub: seriously tacking climate change will entail vast, and to many people unwelcome, changes in lifestyle: abandonment of the private car, much less air travel, extending the useful life of products, recycling rather than abandoning obsolete articles of use, reducing meat consumption, genuinely protecting wilderness areas that are absolutely not available for "development". This is at the individual level, but at least two other levels are also involved. One of these is the fraught question of whether, on the principle that "the polluter pays", the industrialized countries have an ethical responsibility toward the victims of the climate change that they have triggered, and in particular as to whether that ethical responsibility should be concretized in the form of financial and technological transfers, vastly increased aid and the accepting of genuine environmental refugees? The other is that, as "industry" is a synonym for "business", it is actually the corporate community that carries the heaviest responsibility, and should according accept and respond to the fact that past or current pursuit of profits (which have also frequently involved exploitative use of non-renewable resources, involvement in deforestation, the promotion of polluting and unnecessary products and even dangerous or unhealthy ones) is at the basis of a great deal of climate change

and greenhouse gas production. Is it then incumbent on industry to curb its own emissions, reduce pollution, pay for the cleaning up of pollution already produced, and move systematically toward the creation of ecologically responsible and socially useful products and services? Clearly, a good ethical case can be made that this should be so. (For further discussion see Gardiner et al. 2010; Skrimshire 2010.)

3. Energy. We live in a highly energy intensive society. Lighting, heating, cooling and powering our endless array of electrical devices—cookers, toasters, microwaves, personal computers, smartphones, radios, televisions. We insist on traveling in energy burning and polluting devices—cars, buses and planes and transporting much of our produce by truck or by sea in large oil-burning cargo ships. The car is in fact one of the least efficient transport devices ever invented, converting most of its fuel to heat, exhaust and water, with only a small proportion being utilized to actually propel a heavy steel, rubber and plastic container with probably only one person inside. We fly—including so-called "binge flying" (the impulsive decision to take cheap flights at short notice just for personal gratification). All this requires prodigious amounts of energy, most of it currently produced by coal, oil, gas or nuclear power, all requiring non-renewable resources, generating substantial pollution and CO_2 emissions and discharging heat and waste into the atmosphere, rivers or the sea. And many of the appliances powered by it are not themselves energy efficient and require long transmission lines across country where much of the generated energy is lost. Yet emphasis on conservation is weak—designing and using energy efficient devices such as LED light sources, simply turning things off, shunning energy guzzling and inefficient devices such as the car, architectural design that utilizes natural light and cooling and which uses less energy in construction and incorporates recycled materials where possible. Such considerations again have ethical implications—the need to change lifestyles and responsible behavior in relation to personal use of energy on the part of individuals, and the commitment of business to good design, the production of socially useful products, lowering energy use in respect of production and distribution and by the end user, and educating consumers about wise-use and disposal (increasingly a responsibility of manufacturers in societies such as Japan). We all know

that renewable energy generation technologies exist—solar, wind, hydro, tidal, biogas, yet relatively little investment of such technologies exists relative to the continuing vast investment in conventional sources. But good signs also exist. The German government for instance, already a leader in promoting renewable energy sources in a large industrial economy, has recently announced that it wishes to phase out the production of all petrol and diesel powered vehicles by 2030 and their entire replacement with electric ones, a plan that will involve not only the development of more efficient and longer range ones than currently exist by the auto industry, but also of course the development of the infrastructure necessary to support such a move—charging stations in particular and the gradual phasing out of filling stations. Here, while government is taking the initiatives, it will be up to industry to respond in the appropriate ways and perhaps to innovate in ways as yet unseen.

4. Food security and Agriculture. Food security lies at the basis of any other kind of security. With rising global population this is even more the case, and with climate change, soil loss through non-ecological practices of either industrial or some forms of traditional agriculture (slash and burn techniques for example) adding new dimensions of risk, it is evident that a great deal of attention and responsible investment should be being devoted to the agricultural sector. Industrial agriculture in particular with its penchant for "factory farming" of chickens, huge feedlots for beef cattle, monoculture of crops over large land areas, and the attractions of genetically modified crops and the extensive use of chemical fertilizers and pesticides, is of course a form of investment, but one that, when integrated with major processed food producers, is highly energy intensive, promotes the extensive use of antibiotics to control diseases among animals and birds often crowded together in extremely unsanitary conditions, generates large amounts of pollution in the form of literally lakes of animal wastes, damages the soil and, paradoxically, often results in foods of little nutritional value. Obesity and malnutrition from overreliance on low quality processed and denatured foods, including the many varieties of "fast food", and associated diseases such as diabetes and high cholesterol which lead to heart problems, are epidemic in some of the most "developed" countries in the world. The issue of food then,

not only a business and political one, but also teems with ethical questions. Is industrial agriculture basically immoral? Do people have the right to good quality, nutritious food, as, indeed, a basic human right? Is the spread of huge agribusiness and the downstream emergence of large supermarket chains with standardized and often unhealthy food products something to be combatted? Is food security both an individual and collective right? All these questions have implications for individual consumption decisions, business and governments, and given the profound cultural significance of food as well as its necessity in sustaining life, an "ethics of food" involving all the stakeholders is highly necessary. And as with energy of course, quite alternative discourse and practices exist—the "Slow Food" movement with its origins in Italy, but now an international one, the growth of farmers' markets, demand for organic produce which in the UK, for example, is forcing even large supermarket chains to stock such foods, the expansion of community supported agriculture, the taking up of farming by former urban professionals, the mushrooming of organic cafes in many Western and Japanese cities, demand for "natural" materials for clothing, and many other initiatives and practices. Of all the areas we have been considering, a case can certainly be made that an ethics of food—its production, processing, nature, consumption and waste—is central both to civilization and to the businesses that largely control those processes in modern societies where subsistence has ceased to be an option for most people. (For an excellent overview of these issues see Roberts 2009.)

These four examples are sufficient to establish the close links between business and certain practices of "development and ethical or unethical practices" and which in turn point on to certain positive principles of an alternative approach, of which I will here enumerate four: real utility, cradle-to-cradle design, ecological, social and economic restoration, and the aesthetic issue of beauty and what I have elsewhere in this book called "visual justice".

1. Vast quantities of essentially useless and resource consuming items are constantly produced by manufacturers. Many of these may actually be harmful to consumers as any reader of the "nutritional" information on cans and packets will have realized. Others are

simply fads catering to a passing fashion, or are designed to lead to yet further consumption, many are non-biodegradable, and others have no useful function, promoted by advertising, very much one of the areas of business that needs very careful ethical scrutiny as regards the truth of claims. The notion that I would like to introduce here is that of *social utility*: the encouragement of production that does not damage the environment, produces objects of beauty and usefulness, which do not undermine existing dimensions of the economy (say, e.g. the marginalization of handloom products by machine-made synthetics, which, being synthetic are usually ultimately oil based), and of advertising and marketing which genuinely extols the virtues of durable and well-designed products that actually enhance the quality of life.

2. Cradle-to-Cradle design refers of course to the design movement that promotes the creation of objects that are not only both functional and beautiful and ecologically responsible in their source materials, but which do not turn into waste and junk at the end of their careers, but can be recycled, disassembled and the components reused for the manufacture of new creations (McDonaugh and Braungart 2002). Much of the cradle-to-cradle movement is concerned with a wider range of issues than just good design, including of course sustainability. These include ecologically and culturally appropriate architecture and its related idea of "Green Architecture" (Bell 2003; Duran and Fajardo 2010; Kishani 2012), design, including objects of daily use (DeKay 2011).
3. The notion of "ecological restoration" has now entered the environmental and sustainability vocabulary, and has in some quarters become a business in itself—a kind of expanded landscape gardening and design. It refers to the recreation, in as close as possible terms, of damaged and decayed landscapes—former mining pits and industrial sites, degraded former forest or prairie land, or any other site wrenched from its former ecological community. Of course, it is not always possible to do complete restoration or even to know exactly what the original environment was like in all its details, but the movement does show an attempt to put back or give back qualities to the environment lost through human activities (Jordan 2012). So far however the parallel case of *economic* restoration has not gained much traction—the idea of, where possible, reestablishing "natural" economies, economies that is whose

valuable features have been destroyed by the advancement of modernization and monetization. Given that economies always embody ways of life, much is to be learned from the study and replication or adoption of features from, economies that have proved to be sustainable and sociologically stable over long periods. The study of economic anthropology is a valuable tool for examining past or existing actual economies and the ways in which they have organized production, distribution and consumption, often based on notions of reciprocity or gift giving rather than on abstract monetary exchange and valuation (Clammer 2015).

4. I have elsewhere (Clammer 2014) introduced the notion of "visual justice": that there is no good reason why the rich should enjoy beauty, but not the poor: the very subject of chapter six below. Associated with this idea is that good design need not be expensive, that architecture can be culturally appropriate and made from local materials, that handmade products can be superior to machine made ones and that access to attractive natural sites, scenery and leisure pursuits likewise need not only be the province of the rich. The concept of "environmental racism" has now become a well-known notion—that it is not only the poor, but also frequently ethnic minorities, who get to live next to the city trash dump, near polluting industries, near dangerous plants (as the Bhopal tragedy so bitterly exemplified) and with ugly surroundings and bad quality housing and exposure to waste, bad quality air and water, toxins of many kinds and high noise levels. None of these things are necessary and all point to less obvious forms of social injustice. Aesthetics has always been as much a branch of philosophy as ethics, and it at this point that they come together, a subject that will be greatly expanded in the following chapter.

The Applied Ethics of Development

The field of what might be called "applied ethics" has burgeoned in recent years a new issues un-thought of in classical philosophical ethics have emerged. One of these has been ethics as it relates to medicine and biology, including such issues as cloning, euthanasia, organ transplants, the definition of clinical death (in many countries the state which must be observed and verified for organ harvesting to be allowed), abortion and genetic modification. An equally expanding field of ethics has been that of environmental ethics, not surprisingly as our slow ecological catastrophe unfolds. Elsewhere ethics has taken on a new salience in relation to jurisprudence and in particular developments in international law such as debates over the definition of "crimes against humanity" and the conditions on which intervention is allowed under the UN concept of the "responsibility to protect" (and not just to intervene after conflict has broken out). These and other emerging areas of concern, just as much as personal ethics, show that such value considerations are vitally necessary components of public discourse. We might indeed coin the term "social ethics" to refer to the new applications of value enquiry into what are truly collective issues, and ones that transcend now outmoded national boundaries. Arms trading, polluting, human trafficking, cybercrime, the neutrality of the sea lanes, space and the status of hitherto uninhabited areas such as Antarctica, are all examples of the new "commons"—issues that do not respect the political boundaries established by past historical developments.

Business law of course exists, and itself represents a code of values and acceptable behavior, and penalties for the violation of such. But what I am arguing for here is not simply a legal framework or set of good behaviors on the part of individual business persons (don't cheat, give full measure, honor contracts, etc.) but a much wider conception of ethics that relates it systematically to the larger planetary issues outlined above. How is this to be done? Here I will outline four paths which I will argue, point both business ethics and development ethics in the right direction.

1. The concept of the "social economy". All economic systems are fundamental in structuring the lifestyles, concepts of time and space, fashions, financial decisions, modes of social interaction, patterns of mobility and forms of subjectivity (how people understand themselves and others, including my sense of self: if I am what I have, then any loss of that substance will greatly and negatively affect my sense of self, but if I have a secure sense of self-independent of material possessions, then their loss, while painful in some respects, does not attack my sense of self- worth. How I evaluate others will in turn be based on this same modality). Obviously, in a capitalist economic system, business decisions will be largely based on the profit motive rather than social utility, and this as we also know can be highly destructive of the environment,

health and interpersonal relationships as new forms of competition and materially based social exclusion emerge. In response to this numerous alternatives have emerged historically and in the contemporary world—Marxism being in a sense the great-grandfather, but with many other "alternative" proposals emerging—cooperative movements, communes of various kinds, local currencies, so-called "sharing economies", direct farm to consumer marketing networks, barter, gift economies, the idea of "Small is Beautiful" associated with the seminal work of Ernst Schumacher (1979) and associated ideas of "Steady State Economies", "Buddhist" economies, the no-growth and radical scaling back ideas of the French alternative economist Serge Latouche (2010), and the rapidly expanding field of Solidarity Economy (Utting 2015). All of these and many others which cannot be listed here (for a further discussion see Clammer 2016: 65–90) can be grouped together under the rubric of "Social Economy", a term referring to the idea that, whereas in the contemporary dominant economic system we as humans largely serve that economy, in reality the economy should serve us. It should in other words be fair, not generate inequalities, provide people with life-enhancing products, services and entertainment and leisure activities, protect and restore the environment rather than damage it, be sustainable and not recklessly use up non-renewable resources for short-term immediate gain, and promote not competition and greed, but rather conviviality, sharing and mutual cooperation. A tall order perhaps, but a not unreasonable one if we are to survive even this century on a habitable Earth, and one toward achieving which myriad experiments already exist (Bakshi 2009; Hawken 2008). The notion of social economy is also taken to refer to businesses which are either non-profit in nature, or which share their profits with their workers and stakeholders, and which specifically aim to provide goods and services of social utility, and, as such, overlap with the NGO sector with which it shares many aims and management structures. In a way, the notion of social economy summarizes what contemporary business should be like, given the planetary crisis of our own manufacture and toward solving which all resources intellectual, technological, political and business, should be directed.

2. Much of the world, and indeed an unacceptably large part, still suffers from what is usually called "underdevelopment". High levels

of poverty, patterns of gender, caste, ethnic and other forms of exclusion, corruption, landlordism, debt labor amounting virtually to slavery, high levels of income inequality within and between nations, radically differential access to health care, education, decent housing and even clean water, still abound in our "globalized" world, in which luxury and overconsumption abounds often quite literally alongside degradation. These circumstances have of course given rise to the whole large field of "development studies" and the policy and practical initiatives arising. But unfortunately business studies and development studies rarely dialogue with each other. This is unfortunate for several reasons. In the so-called "developing world" questions of business and questions of development are closely related, whether in terms of the very business environment itself (if there even is one), quality and availability of labor, what kind of market exists and how to reach it with what kinds of products, and of course the list of ethical questions: should one attempt to sell sugary, non-nutritious drinks while not only using up the local groundwater to manufacture it, but knowing that it has no health value, contributes to dental problems and diabetes, and is expensive in terms of average local incomes? As we know from experience, there are indeed companies that have done exactly that, a situation that raises both ethical questions and ones related to development—is this the kind of product needed, or is it one that just fuels more poverty, an addiction to unhealthy products and has no social utility at all (except to the profit line of the manufacturer)? At this point, business ethics and what has become known as development ethics converge (Goulet 2006; Gasper 2004), and so they should, as my recommendation here is that they enter into close dialogue with one another.

3. Two large issues face any social or economic enterprise in the contemporary situation—notably sustainability and transition. The former of course refers to the facts that we are rapidly making our (only) planet uninhabitable, or if habitable highly degraded, ugly, resource-poor, without many of the species that have inhabited it for eons, and hot. Since under these conditions business-as-usual should be unthinkable, the alternative, and a highly urgent one, is to turn all our attention to creating a sustainable future. If we do not of course we will not have a future. There is, tragically, already a lot of evidence that we have trapped ourselves in the form of

self-destructive path-dependency that Jared Diamond has identified as leading to civilizational collapse over long stretches of past history, and which almost always have resulted from the willful destruction of the environment and resource base on which those civilizations were dependent (Diamond 2005). If, as we have suggested, business activities are the source of many of our planetary problems, then the future, if it is to be sustainable, requires sustainable business practices. This may involve some radical ideas given the presuppositions of our current economic and business systems, including not only the unthinkable idea for many of "degrowth" as promoted by Serge Latouche, but also perhaps slightly less unpalatable ideas such as that of "Prosperity without Growth" advanced by the British economist Tim Jackson (2010). At the base of many of these ideas is the simple and obvious one that we live on a finite planet. Growth cannot continue forever. And this is another point at which business ethics and development ethics converge: for the rich economies to slow down is one thing; for poor economies to be told to stop growing is altogether another. Perhaps the most radical challenge for development thinking is to devise plans that will eradicate the evils of underdevelopment while not committing developing societies to the same path of overconsumption, resource exploitation, pollution and environmental destruction as the overdeveloped, not an easy political message to communicate, but a very necessary one. The problem of "transition" in the highly developed economies may be one of managing energy decline, but in the less developed it will be the equally challenging problem of creating a model of development in which high energy use is not at all an option, while still facing the challenges of poverty, illiteracy and lack of access to basic social resources.

4. In the business schools of my acquaintance, and possibly in ones of development studies too, the notion of "leadership" is much talked about. But such leadership is naturally defined as within the existing economic/business environment. This model may be now not only out of date, but positively dangerous. It may, in other words, lead people into reproducing exactly the behavior that has got us into trouble in the first place. Rather, new concepts of leadership, whether in business, development, politics, law and related spheres of public service, are needed together with a new image of the

contemporary hero. Judging by the extent of the mindless violence which TV and film producers do not seem to be able to extend their feeble minds beyond, it seems that very old notions of the hero are still very much extant—the violent warrior who, while he may be fighting evil in some form, does so though the destructive and death-dealing means hardly different from his opponents (with apologies to Superman). Today new forms of leaders and heroes are urgently needed that break with the old, basically military, pattern. As Sara Parkin has thoughtfully argued, leadership today should be for sustainability (Parkin 2010). To nurture such a leadership implies new forms of transformative education, including, or perhaps especially in business schools, and new images of doing business, linking it specifically to the needs of sustainability, not only in the minimal sense of having a livable future, but in a much more positive sense of actively *creating* that desirable future. Far from being approached with fear and trepidation, such as vocation should be the most intellectually exciting and challenging that can be imagined—a true statement of the new leadership in fact.

Shaping Futures

The future, as futures always are, is inevitable. The question is what we want to make of it. The thrust of this paper has been that business, being at the root of many of our contemporary problems—environmental ones, resource extraction, pollution, overconsumption at least—is also, if not *the* solution, certainly one of the most important ones. Integral to this argument has been the centrality of business ethics, not simply in its more traditional sense, but in a truly planetary context. The planet cannot be saved or restored to habitability without a new concept and practice of business, one oriented to both an "Earth Ethics" and a "Development Ethics", with sustainability and life-enhancement as the goal. Such a vision is no longer utopian: it is now a necessity. Humans make their own societies, so it is up to us to create the future that we collectively want. If we want the current one, we are headed for civilizational destruction, even though the Earth itself will survive (in fact quite well without us). If we want a different one then we have to rigorously and urgently rethink our systems of economics, politics and value systems. This requires both very practical thinking and a new social ethics of care, responsibility, recognition of mutual interdependence, and willingness to transfer technology, aid and expertise to those most affected by the mess we have made of our beautiful nest. This is what the eco-theologian Thomas Berry has called the "Great Work" of our generation (Berry 1999), and so it is. The nature of business and the education of future business leaders lies at the basis of this transformation, and such an education must be framed within the context of the pursuit of cultural rights.

References

Bakshi, Rajni. 2009. *Bazaars, Conversations and Freedom: For a Market Culture Beyond Greed and Fear*. New Delhi: Penguin Books.

Bell, Bryan. 2003. *Good Deeds, Good Design: Community Service Through Architecture*. Princeton, NJ: Princeton Architectural Press.

Berry, Thomas. 1999. *The Great Work: Our Way into the Future*. New York: Bell Tower.

Clammer, John. 2014. *Vision and Society: Towards a Sociology and Anthropology from Art*. London and New York: Routledge.

Clammer, John. 2015. Social Economics and Economic Anthropology: Challenging Conventional Economic Thinking and Practice. In *Social Economy in China and the World*, ed. Ngai Pun, Ben Hok-Bun Ku, Hairong Yan, and Anita Koo, 3–16. London and New York: Routledge.

Clammer, John. 2016. *Cultures of Transition and Sustainability*. Basingstoke and New York: Palgrave Macmillan.

Curry, Patrick. 2011. *Ecological Ethics: An Introduction*. Cambridge: Polity Press.

DeKay, Mark. 2011. *Integral Sustainable Design: Transformative Perspectives*. London and New York: Routledge.

Diamond, Jared. 2005. *Collapse: How Societies Choose to Fail or Succeed*. New York: Penguin.

Duran, Sergi Costa, and Julio Fajardo. 2010. *The Sourcebook of Contemporary Green Architecture*. New York: Collins Design.

Gardiner, Stephen M., Simon Caney, Dale Jamieson, and Henry Shue (eds.). 2010. *Climate Ethics: Essential Readings*. Oxford: Oxford University Press.

Gasper, Des. 2004. *The Ethics of Development*. Edinburgh: Edinburgh University Press.

Goulet, Denis. 2006. *Development Ethics at Work: Explorations*. London and New York: Routledge.

Hawken, Paul. 2008. *Blessed Unrest: How the Largest Social Movement in History Is Restoring Grace, Justice and Beauty to the World*. New York: Penguin Books.

Hopkins, Bob. 2008. *The Transition Handbook: From Oil Dependency to Local Resilience*. White River Junction, VT: Chelsea Green Publishing.

Jackson, Tim. 2010. *Prosperity Without Growth: Economics for a Finite Planet*. London and Washington, DC: Earthscan.
Jordan, William R. 2012. *The Sunflower Forest: Ecological Restoration and the New Communion with Nature*. Berkeley and London: University of California Press.
Kishani, Nirmal. 2012. *Greening Asia: Emerging Principles for Sustainable Architecture*. Singapore: BCI Asia.
Latouche, Serge. 2010. *Farewell to Growth*, trans. David Macey. Cambridge and Malden, MA: Polity Press.
McDonaugh, William, and Michael Braungart. 2002. *Cradle to Cradle: Remaking the Way We Make Things*. New York: North Point Press.
Parkin, Sara. 2010. *The Positive Deviant: Sustainability Leadership in a Perverse World*. London and Washington, DC: Earthscan.
Roberts, Paul. 2009. *The End of Food*. Boston and New York: Mariner Books.
Schumacher, E.F. 1979. *Small Is Beautiful: A Study of Economics as If People Mattered*. London: Abacus.
Skrimshire, Stefan (ed.). 2010. *Future Ethics: Climate Change and Apocalyptic Imagination*. London and New York: Continuum.
Urry, John. 2013. *Societies Beyond Oil: Oil Dregs and Social Futures*. London and New York: Zed Books.
Utting, Peter (ed.). 2015. *Social and Solidarity Economy: Beyond the Fringe*. London and New York: Zed Books in Association with the United Nations Research Institute for Social Development (UNRISD).

CHAPTER 4

Is Multiculturalism the Answer? Global Ethics and the Dialectic of the Universal and the Particular

One possible approach to the existence of cultural diversity and of the demands that all cultures be "heard"—accorded recognition and the right to protection and expression—is to stress the value of multiculturalism. But this seemingly totally positive concept has its problems, and is a frequently contested one. As becomes quickly apparent, it is politically charged, with a variety of meanings to different actors, and often carries a heavy ideological baggage (Ivison 2010). This chapter will explore some of these issues and will suggest that it does have utility in the context of debates about both cultural rights and holistic development if understood in a way that links cultural diversity to rights and social ethics in a way that genuinely advances the recognition of the authenticity of cultures and their claims to visibility and respect. Global changes indeed intensify the need for genuine multiculturalism as older liberal conceptions of multiculturalism are increasingly challenged by emerging patterns of cultural hybridity fueled by immigration of peoples of a different ethnic and religious composition from many "receiving" countries and as debates about such issues as a "politics of difference" or of "post-identity politics" proliferate in the academy and the wider marketplace of ideas and policy.

For some commentators, multiculturalism is an ideal, rather than a description of existing reality. For, as the philosopher John Dewey suggested some time ago, the existence of cultural pluralism is not necessarily an obstacle to creating a genuinely democratic society, but also a valuable resource. Certainly the world *is* culturally diverse, and despite

J. Clammer, *Cultural Rights and Justice*,
https://doi.org/10.1007/978-981-13-2811-4_4

pressures toward homogenization, a high level of diversity is unlikely to disappear, even under the regime of globalization. The question then arises of the relationship between this actually existing cultural diversity and the desire to seek universalism in key values (as reflected in the Universal Declaration of Human Rights) and to find common approaches to our pressing global problems. Where might one start to look for these commonalities and shared problem-solving approaches?

I will suggest that there are three possible starting points that to a great extent transcend cultural differences, while allowing for the full flourishing of cultural diversity. The first of these is ecology, a field increasingly providing a common ground—one that impacts the whole globe and all peoples, and which for the most part (leaving aside the climate change deniers) is non-ideological and trans-religious. An aspect of this is what some scholars have called the "ecological self"—the recognition that the human species does not stand alone or at the apex of some evolutionary sequence, but is one species among many, and that we are totally dependent physically and psychologically on the rest of the biosphere that we are privileged to inhabit and share with other life forms (Macy 1990; Clammer 2018). This requires that we find a notion of human identity that transcends anthropomorphism and forces us to recognize that even culture has a larger context—nature. The eco-philosopher Warwick Fox has raised and attempted to answer the question "what is wrong with anthropocentrism?" in philosophical terms (its conceptual inadequacy as a complete explanation of humanity's place in the total world or even cosmic system), its damaging empirical consequences (seen in its all-too-visible consequences for all life on the planet), and in terms of ethics (the hubris of assuming the convenient, self-serving and comfortable—but entirely unverifiable—position that we humans are, in our present conflictual and environmentally destructive form, the end point of evolution). On the basis of this critique, Fox goes on to suggest that the achievement of a sense of self that extends beyond a narrow ego-centered view of personality leads to three more expanded sense of identity—what he calls the personal, the ontological and the cosmological, which he characterizes as follows: "Personally based identification refers to experiences of commonality with other entities that are brought about through personal involvement with those entities…Ontologically based identification refers to experiences of commonality with all that is brought about through deep-seated realization of the fact *that* things are… Cosmologically based identification refers to experiences of commonality with all that are brought about through deep-seated realization of the fact that we and all other entities are aspects of a single unfolding reality. This realization can be brought about through the empathic incorporation of *any* cosmology (i.e. any fairly comprehensive account of *how* the world is) that sees the world as a single unfolding process—as a 'unity in progress' to employ Theodore Roszak's splendid phrase" (Fox 1990: 249–252).

The second is the unifying theme of this book—the requirement of justice. Simply to recognize the existence or desirability of cultural diversity is insufficient, since cultures often contain or conceal inequalities, hierarchies of power and domination, traditionally sanctioned forms of gender discrimination, ageism or racism, and ecologically damaging practices. The subtle task of cultural critique and appreciation is to both recognize that different cultural expressions are equally valid attempts to grasp the complexity of the world and to impose some meaning on it, and to encourage the flourishing of those cultural expressions while urging their evolution toward congruity with larger existential desiderata such as ecological sustainability, non-violence, respect for other life forms, internal social and cultural justice and tolerance of cultural expressions (e.g. religions) other than their own. Given that all cultures are historical and contingent, all can change. What it does not have to be the only possibility. Those cultures and civilizations that have violated the larger ecological and existential limits have brought about their own self-destruction, a path that we too may well be on (Diamond 2006). Globalization, as we now well know, has not brought about a planetary regime of equality, justice and abundance for all. Far from it, it has often brought about the destruction of indigenous cultures, exacerbated inequalities within and between nations, promoted the free flow of capital while both triggering and restricting the free movement of peoples, and is behind many of the resource depletion and environmental problems now plaguing the globe. Cultural diversity without social justice is hollow: worse it can become an ideological and conceptual smoke screen behind which inequalities can flourish, and "universalism" means simply the hegemony of the powerful.

The third is the principle of interconnectedness, not only of humans with the rest of nature, but the dense interconnections between social and cultural processes themselves. As we now again well know, and this reflected in the constant calls for "interdisciplinary" studies in universities and elsewhere, conventional academic disciplinary boundaries while they certainly help to focus attention on particular aspects of the whole, also tend to conceal the real interrelationships between the parts that make up that whole. While a "theory of everything" is hard in practice to come by, given the complexity of that everything, much can be learnt from attempts to do so, whether via such means as complexity theory, through the search for holism in fragmented but vital fields such as development studies (Schieffer and Lessem 2014), in the newly emerging field of "Big History" (Rodrigue et al. 2017) or in the thinking of such unclassifiable thinkers as Ken Wilber (2000). All this points to what the theologian and environmentalist Thomas Berry has called the "Great Work" of our generation (Berry 1999), or what David Korten has characterized as opposing what he terms "Empire"—the seeking for domination rather than partnership in relation to both nature and human beings, the allowing of the economic to become not our tool, but our master, the emergence of consumerism and materialism as means of attempting to establish our identities and statuses, and the imperial ambitions of some religions, in stark contrast to the goals of their founders to promote community, sociality and compassion (Korten 2006).

This is where the notion of the "ecological self" again proves to have salience. Such as understanding of the relationship of the personal self to the wider universe has sociological and political implications, especially when linked to emerging alternative notions of citizenship. The very notion of citizenship in its classical sense has come to be challenged with the advent of contemporary forms of globalization, and with it the weakening of the actual power of the nation-state, the emergence of new cross-border actors such as transnational corporations, international NGOs and multilateral agencies such as the World Bank and the WTO, and new forms of transnational practice such as the widespread use of the internet, mass tourism and the spread of many forms of popular culture across national boundaries. Julie Davidson argues that there are two major discourses shaping emerging ideas of planetary rather than national citizenship—notably globalization and sustainability (Davidson 2004: 168). While globalization refers to the linkages (positive or negative) that currently bind the world into what is effectively a single system, sustainability draws our attention to the fact that the current system has no future in that it is fundamentally self-destructive. Unless that is, means are found to create a global or planetary conception of citizenship based on mutual social responsibilities on the one hand, and collective responsibilities to nature on the other.

An idea that brings together the notions of the ecological self and citizenship is what Bart van Steenbergen (1994) has called "ecological citizenship". The traditional notion of citizenship is one of a formal entitlement based on such criteria as place of birth, is now being challenged by the idea of its being an active and ethical status implying obligations and responsibilities, including very much responsibilities toward the environment, and suggesting that a cosmopolitan identity is today the only realistic and moral social location of a global citizen. While *rights* continue to occupy their place of central importance, these are balanced by the significance of parallel *responsibilities* and the sensible use of freedoms. Such a notion of citizenship involves not only a notion of political identity, but also the dimension of environmental responsibility, and one in which, while local identities related to specific places, cultures, ethnicities and religions remain salient, these are all located within the larger frame of a transnational model. As Davidson again puts it "At the core of a cosmopolitan ethic is the idea of people taking more *responsibility* for the conditions of other people's lives. Cosmopolitan citizenship is premised on cooperative relationships that enable the sharing of responsibilities and burdens. Like it or not, this era of global risk and vulnerability makes fellow citizens of people across the globe because of their shared responsibilities to participate in the achievement of collective goods such as environmental protection and equity. Citizenship for sustainability entails responsibilities not just for those goods necessary for immediate survival, but also for those collective goods that enable the flourishing of humans and other species now and into the future" (Davidson 2004: 176).

But how, given the still virtual monopoly of nation-states on the granting or withholding of citizenship is this to be achieved? It is certainly possible to conceive of two "levels" of citizenship—that conferred by traditional, if weakening, nation-states, and a broader and more inclusive conception shared by large numbers of people in a "virtual" but still real transnational space, something in a minor sense already true of staff of international organizations such as the United Nations. But however it might be achieved in practice, underlying such a notion are a number of fundamental principles. Initially we can identify at least three of these. The first is the development of an institutional framework for global governance and ensuring the public accountability of the major multilateral actors including transnational corporations. The second is the severe curtailing of consumption and extraction levels in favor of more appropriate practices and values for the achievement of sustainability. The third is the formulation of a global ethic. Intervention then must take place at the political, social and cultural levels simultaneously.

A global ethic as of now clearly exists as an ideal rather than as a reality, although many elements of one already exist embodied in such instruments as the Charter of the United Nations, the Universal Declaration of Human Rights, and the Earth Charter, and many other such documents and declarations. Naturally, no progress can be made toward the realization of a global ethic unless the idea is enunciated and thought given to strategies for its realization. Here some conceptual clarification is useful. Values and ethics, while closely related, are not identical: one may well hold values that are not expressed in what would seem to be either expected ethical behaviors or anticipated cultural outcomes. I may believe in the sanctity of life, but still eat meat, even if not of other humans. My government may be a signatory of the UDHR but still violate rights within its borders. The state to which I belong may hold itself up to the rest of the world as a paragon of justice, rights and freedoms, but still refuse to recognize the jurisdiction of the International Criminal Court or to sign the UN Treaty banning landmines (and may also be one of the world's biggest arms dealers, along with other permanent members of the UN Security Council). The first requirement of a global ethic would be the avoidance of hypocrisy in the search for values upon which more or less universal agreement across cultures, religions and political systems can be reached—something proved to be possible by the long consultative process involved in the drafting and eventual adoption of the Earth Charter. The second is to inculcate through education, socialization, cultural practice and the law, the idea that there should be no gap between values and practice, between that which is affirmed and that which is actually done on the world arena.

Many of the conflicts between cultures cannot be attributed to material sources (such as resource competition) alone. They also involve the ontologies that shape practice and appear in any society as the *doxa* or unspoken or taken-for-granted assumptions on which any culture operates. Such ontologies are not only or even principally cognitive in nature, but involve different conceptions of nature, different conceptions of the body—appearing in many indirect forms such as in laws pertaining to censorship and the socially permissible at any given point of time in art and the media (Young 2005), and different cosmologies. These usually arise from indigenous but not always articulated conceptions or intuitions of land, health and healing, food, aesthetics, symbolism, clothing and other cultural elements that, while not initially appearing to have any bearing on ethics, in fact at deep levels most certainly do so. Diet, for example, relates directly to numerous other aspects of culture including religion, body image, conceptions of what may legitimately be taken from nature and in what quantities and yet further aspects of cultural identity. These are all parts of what might be thought of as a contextualized ethics—locally rooted understandings of correct behavior toward others, non-human beings (as surfaces in debates about the rights of animals), and apparently inanimate nature—apparently because the notion of the inanimate is itself a matter of cultural and religious decision and local ethnoscience (Clammer et al. 2004).

Such a concern with the local is not to deny the possibility of non-coercive universals (ones that do not illegitimately "flatten out" actual variations and create illegitimate hegemony of one particular thought system), or to be reduced to the position of cultural relativism. It is to argue rather that both commonalities as well as cultural (including linguistic) diversity is socially important in the same way that biodiversity is ecologically important to exist in a kind of dialectical relationship with one another, as do rights and responsibilities. Universals in this context mean less the ones identified by anthropologists as such (kinship, religion, art, the incest taboo and so forth), than ones rooted in our common existential condition as humans, our common location in nature as a species equally dependent on the benevolence of the biosphere, and the fact that, as Noam Chomsky has demonstrated for language, there is, despite surface linguistic diversity, a "deep grammar"—a logical and communicative set of structures that make translation between all languages possible. Such a view is echoed by structural anthropologists such as Claude Levi-Strauss, who has argued that all cultural variations emanate from a large but finite set of possibilities, set in large part by our environment, and many biologists who argue that we share with other bio-forms natural limits (longevity, nutritional needs and so forth) and social ones (the need for company and communication with others of our species), and to a great extent, with other species too (Wilson 1982).

But while biology potentially provides one line of approach to the question of the existence and qualities of a supposedly universal human nature, political science suggests another, and one less enmeshed in the kinds of controversies that surround any kind of sociobiology. In a survey of arguments pertaining to the idea of a human nature from this latter perspective, Christopher Berry proposes that in reality the discussion must go far beyond politics to embrace all of the human sciences, since the topic is central to a range of debates including human rights, the perfectability of humans, freedom versus constraint, and the possibility of a universalist political theory or one of international law (Berry 1986). To even begin to address this range of issues, Berry finds it necessary to call on anthropology to inform more conventional political theory. This is partly because the problem of relativism is as acute in political science as it is in cultural studies, maybe more so as the whole possibility of establishing a universal code of human rights hangs on the ability to agree on a reasonable concept of the unity of the human species, as too do the understandings of "development" enshrined in such documents as the UN's Millennium Development Goals (MDGs) and their successor the Sustainable Development Goals (SDGs). As Berry and others have pointed out, whether this purported unity is posited on the basis of biosocial limitations, the logical requirements of rationality, or the intertranslatability of all languages, actually matters less than the requirement to *find* or *assert* such a structure (Berry 1986: 77). There are actually three different questions here. The first is the empirical existence (or not) of a universal human nature, which, if it exists must have as its basis shared values, since to be biologically human but to have no moral values would call into serious question one's humanity. The second is the grounds on which we argue for or against such a unity (possession of language? Kinship? Universality of art?). The third is the quite different question of whether or not it *matters* if we can establish a conception of human unity or not. We might, for example, whether for ecological, political, aesthetic political or anthropological grounds, *wish* to believe in the sisterhood and brotherhood of all humankind because that belief works a lot better than its alternatives in promoting a peaceful, just and pleasant world, and because for this reason we *want* to bring that unity into existence. In that case, it may not matter if "human nature" objectively exists. Perhaps to create such a unity is our evolutionary goal.

This latter position indeed seems to be that of the philosopher Richard Rorty whose defense of liberalism is based on the idea that human solidarity or community is all that is necessary (Rorty 1982): common human nature, and that as a result pragmatism is the appropriate philosophical position: "loyalty to our fellow humans does not require something permanent and ahistorical…which guarantees convergence to agreement" (Rorty 1982: 171). This view would be contested by many others, including Marx and those who have followed him to various degrees, not by arguing for an ahistorical essence, but rather by arguing that humanity is less a given than something created by its own labor. We have a "species being", as do all other bio-forms, but this being is, at least up to a point, elastic and amendable, and history is less the story of our continuity as a species than that of our self-formation through labor. David Harvey has undertaken a contemporary elaboration of this, including its implications for our responsibilities to nature, our utopian impulses, the relation between self-fashioning and justice, and the geographical rather than the biological boundaries of being human (Harvey 2002).

The "anti-humanism" of Michel Foucault and Levi-Strauss, which appears at first sight as attempts to demolish the idea of a human nature, prove on closer examination to be something rather different. In rooting their analyses in ethnology—one of the "counter-sciences" that, together with psychoanalysis, "ceaselessly 'unmake' that very man who is creating and recreating his positivity… One may say of both of them what Levi-Strauss said of ethnology: that they dissolve man" (Foucault 1966: 379–381). Both thinkers are attacking the forms of idealist philosophical anthropology stemming from Kant, and suggesting rather a view of the human rooted in actual struggles for recognition and survival in a material world, constrained by biological limits, while striving endlessly for creativity and meaning. For creativity is clearly not confined to the arts: an equally important aspect of the human imagination is social creativity—the ability to invent new social forms—and the ability to achieve a moral imagination and to strive for self-transcendence. All these contain the possibility of an open future that we can collectively shape, and of what Roberto Mangabeira Unger (2001) has called a "non-necessitarian" social theory—one beyond determinism, yet within the bounds of the reality of the world that we have been given.

Cultural Diversity and Global Ethics

Cultural diversity is not only an empirical reality, but also a desired and potential state of an enriching pluralism. But how then it be reconciled with the idea of a global ethics? This issue was addressed in the forum of the 1993 Parliament of the World's Religions and the result enshrined in the concluding deliberations of that congress. In the preface to the final Declaration of the Parliament, the editors state that "By a global ethic we do not mean a global ideology or a single unified religion beyond all existing religions, and certainly not the domination of one religion over all others. By a global ethic we mean a fundamental consensus on binding values, irrevocable standards and personal attitudes" (Kung and Kuschel 1993: 21). In practice, the Declaration suggests this means the humane treatment of all beings and the recognition of the inalienable dignity of all humans regardless of age, race, gender, religion, social origin, physical or mental ability. This, it is asserted, arise from four fundamental guidelines found in most of the world's religions in some form: commitment to a culture of non-violence and respect for life; commitment to a culture of solidarity and a just economic order; commitment to a culture of tolerance and a life of truthfulness; and commitment to a culture of equal rights and partnership between men and women (Kung and Kuschel 1993: 24).

Apart from the actual proposals of the Declaration, two other things are noteworthy—the basis of shared values in *culture*, with the added dimension that this culture is an emerging and dynamic one, not to be simply equated with any actually existing specific culture, and the recognition that a *just economy* is one of the major bases of any shared ethic. While religion may shape values at one level of culture, the economy is often busy undoing them at another and substituting its own, and most often it is the economy that wins. Civilizational dialogue today is also structured largely through economic relations and few would realistically disagree that the WTO has far more influence on our daily lives than the Parliament of the World's Religions. Economic factors must then be recognized as primary determinants of culture in the civilizational patterns that we have allowed to emerge globally since the Industrial Revolution and so must be themselves transformed if progress toward a workable global ethic is to be made (Muzaffar 2005).

Multiple cultural identities are fragile and even temporary: they require a supportive socioeconomic environment for their survival and flourishing. Such an awareness not only inspires the various UNESCO declarations on the protection of cultural diversity, but also reflects the fact that cultures are *performative*—they must be remembered, repeated, expressed and transmitted. This cannot happen when cultures are suppressed deliberately or undermined by homogenizing styles of globalization, where indigenous languages are forbidden, or one's art, literature or fashions denigrated. A matter of cultural rights is consequently not only protection, but also the deconstruction of the hierarchical categories that separate "high" from "popular" culture, "arts" from "crafts" (Buszek 2011).

We are then dealing with a dialectical process, one in which global citizenship possesses a local rooting, and in which globalization itself has a tendency to trigger movements toward localization and the pursuit of the authenticity of indigenous cultures. There has been a tendency in much recent social philosophy, cultural theory and anthropology to talk about the "Other" as the counterpoint to the self, drawing in large part from the philosophies of Martin Buber and Emmanuel Levinas. From this some commentators have derived a politics of "difference" often promoting a multiculturalism of separation rather than of communication, a model often extending the gender (e.g. Irigaray 1989). But the pursuit of universalism in the sense of a global ethic affirming diversity while recognizing commonalities requires a new philosophical anthropology, one in which there are no "Others" in any ethical sense, and one in which the politics and sociology of difference is transcended by one of unity. This position however can easily slip quietly into an idealist one. But in discussing ethics it is always necessary to consider its shadow side and the reason for which ethics needs to exist—notably the existence of evil.

This of course is an enormous topic that has preoccupied philosophers and theologians for centuries. As Tzvetan Todorov has pointed out, collective identities are fragile, and the "clash of civilizations" debate signals deeper fears about the barbarism that exists within and between civilizations, and the severe limitations of idealist accounts of "dialogue between civilizations" that do not take into account the actual dynamics of intercultural relations and the political and economic forces that drive them (Todorov 2010). For identity politics may actually stand in the way of democratic and genuinely liberatory processes if they are based on difference rather than dialogue, and can and do become the means through which tensions rather than consensus emerge (Gilbert 2010). So whereas idealism in its philosophical sense can be naïve in the complex globalized and politicized world that we inhabit, idealism in an ethical sense is necessary since without goals and even utopias, standards cannot be set toward which social, political, economic, artistic and religious systems and institutions should strive. As suggested, the UDHR, the Earth Charter and attempts to create a Universal Charter of Human Responsibilities (Kumar and Sudha 2010) all represent moves in this positive direction, and equality and justice between cultures as well as within them need to be one of these goals.

This is vividly illustrated by current debates about climate justice. It is presumably now the consensus that it has been the rich industrial nations that have through their economic and consumption practices that are the main culprits in creating global warming and all its attendant and destructive effects. But it is the poorer and still largely agricultural nations of the global South that are most likely to feel the effects and have less resources to combat them. Should then the North increase aid and compensation to the South to help mitigate these effects? Or perhaps even more painfully, should the North accept that it has to make drastic cuts in consumption, lifestyle expectations and energy use to help the globe as a whole while increasing the transfer of resources to the South? The controversies that these issues are creating will certainly move issues of environmental justice to the forefront of intercultural and inter-civilizational debates in the coming decade or more. This is not only because of the severity of the issues, but also because it is environmental questions that are now forming the common ground on which intercultural debate can take place. A sign of this is the way that environmentalism has encouraged religions across the spectrum to address the resources within their own traditions that speak to this deep ecological crisis and to help revise values in ways that promote sustainability and responsibility toward the Earth (e.g. Gottlieb 2004, 2006). The Earth Charter, a secular document that in its formulation process drew on multiple sources, voices, traditions and cultural experiences, is an excellent model for approaching the issue of cultural universalism and particularism at many levels—in its process of consultation, conclusions, methodology and its realism. The first element—consultation—relates to its seeking a universal set of values for our conflicted world: "The Earth Charter" focuses attention on the need for global ethics. It is concerned with the identification and promotion of ethical values that are widely shared by all nations, cultures, and religions—what some philosophers call universal values. Global ethics are of critical importance in the Great Transition because we live in an increasingly interdependent, fragile, and complex world…global interdependence means that no community or nation can manage its problems by itself. Partnership and collaboration are essential (Steven C. Rockefeller quoted in Corcoran and Wohlpart 2008: xv).

The second element demonstrated that a universal consensus on values could indeed be reached through a long process of consultation and drafting involving people from many cultures, religions, and ethnicities, of both genders, and of many kinds of social, professional and educational backgrounds. This proved to skeptics that with goodwill and attentive listening, agreement could be achieved. The third was to recognize the critical and perilous time in which we live, in which real and urgent choices must be made—to enhance life, promote partnership and to create an integrated set of ethics and practices to address the contemporary crisis and to challenge the forces of "Empire"—greed, violence, lack of care for nature. If one looks for a model that combines idealism with realism, a methodology for achieving consensus, and a synthesis of ecological care and social justice, the Earth Charter is a good place to begin.

The question of values is then hopefully clear enough—the need for a global ethic based on agreed and shared principles for enhancing a just and ecologically responsible life on this planet. Development ethicist Denis Goulet expresses this very clearly—that rather than having two streams of concern—with protecting nature on the one hand and seeking economic and social justice on the other—they both need to merge since "This dissonance is tragic because it is the identical pseudo-development which lies at the root of both problems. The only antidote to pseudo-development is a working ethic of what is generally called 'sustainable development' but which is better termed 'integral authentic development'. Such an ethic joins the two normative streams, linking concern with environmental responsibility with the drive for universal economic justice. There can be no sound development ethic without environmental wisdom, and, conversely, no environmental wisdom without a solid development ethic" (Goulet 1995: 119). Goulet in turn traces this fatal dichotomy not only to the absence of a common ethic, but also to the non-functional and non-responsive nature of many of our current institutions: "In rich and poor countries alike, still another major obstacle blocks the quest for new development models: the worldwide paralysis of creative imagination. Although new institutions and problem-solving approaches are urgently needed, the well-springs of social invention have run dry...today's global institutions are relics of an earlier age and no longer function. They are already dead, but not yet buried" (Goulet 1995: 185). While I feel that Goulet is over pessimistic here—the well-springs of imagination have certainly not run dry—he is correct in that it is often, perhaps usually, that those springs or the flow from them are indeed blocked by moribund institutions. Hence as he also argues, the need for alternative ones, ones that are actually responsive to the gravity of the problems that confront us.

This becomes in a sense a question of methodology. Proclaiming a global ethics or a universal charter of either or both of human rights or human responsibilities is one thing; seeing it widely or universally practiced is another. As the distinguished Catholic liberation theologian Leonardo Boff rightly puts it "Having a new cosmology is not enough. How are we to spread it and bring people to internalize it so as to inspire new behaviors, nourish new dreams, and bolster a new kindness toward the Earth? That is certainly a pedagogical challenge" (Boff 1997: 119). All this suggests a number of thoughts toward the future. One is to indeed bolster and encourage the imagination, and specifically the social imagination. Insofar as society is constructed by the humans who inhabit it, so it can be changed, its great inertia notwithstanding. Another is the need to constantly engage with and challenge globalization itself as the source of many of the ills, under the rubric of "development" that currently afflict the planet. Third is the nurturing of new institutions that actually enshrine in practice the global ethics that we are speaking of here, and the creating of new stories that embody them, themes to which we will return.

References

Berry, Christopher J. 1986. *Human Nature*. London: Macmillan.

Berry, Thomas. 1999. *The Great Work: Our Way into the Future*. New York: Bell Tower.

Boff, Leonardo. 1997. *Cry of the Earth, Cry of the Poor*. Maryknoll, NY: Orbis Books.

Buszek, Maria Elena (ed.). 2011. *Extra/Ordinary: Craft and Contemporary Art*. Durham, NC and London: Duke University Press.

Clammer, John. 2018. Cosmopolitanism Beyond Anthropocentrism: The Ecological Self and Transcivilizational Dialogue. In *Beyond Cosmopolitanism: Towards Planetary Transformation*, ed. A.K. Giri, 33–51. New York and Basingstoke: Palgrave Macmillan.

Clammer, John, Sylvie Poirier, and Eric Schwimmer (eds.). 2004. *Figured Worlds: Ontological Obstacles in Intercultural Relations*. Toronto and London: Toronto University Press.

Corcoran, Peter Blaze, and A. James Wohlpart (eds.). 2008. *A Voice for the Earth*. Athens, GA and London: University of Georgia Press.

Davidson, Julie. 2004. Citizenship and Sustainability: Rights and Responsibilities in the Global Age. In *Controversies in Environmental Sociology*, ed. Rob White, 168–184. Cambridge: Cambridge University Press.

Diamond, Jared. 2006. *Collapse: How Societies Choose to Fail or Succeed*. New York: Penguin Books.

Foucault, Michel. 1966. *The Order of Things: An Archaeology of the Human Sciences*, trans. Alan Sheridan. New York: Vintage.

Fox, Warren. 1990. *Towards a Transpersonal Ecology: New Foundations for Environmentalism*. Boston and London: Shambhala.

Gilbert, Paul. 2010. *Cultural Identity and Political Ethics*. Edinburgh: Edinburgh University Press.

Gottlieb, Roger S. (ed.). 2004. *This Sacred Earth: Religion, Nature, Environment*. London and New York: Routledge.

Gottlieb, Roger S. 2006. *A Greener Faith: Religious Environmentalism and Our Planet's Future*. New York and Oxford: Oxford University Press.

Goulet, Denis. 1995. *Development Ethics: A Guide to Theory and Practice*. New York and London: Apex Press and Zed Books.

Harvey, David. 2002. *Spaces of Hope*. Edinburgh: Edinburgh University Press.

Irigaray, Luce. 1989. *Les temps de la difference*. Paris: Le Livre de Poche.

Ivison, Duncan (ed.). 2010. *The Ashgate Research Companion to Multiculturalism*. Farnham: Ashgate.

Korten, David C. 2006. *The Great Turning: From Empire to Earth Community*. Bloomfield, CT and San Francisco: Kumarian Press: Berrett-Koehler.

Kumar, Jeevan, and S. Sudha (eds.). 2010. *Uniting in Responsibilities in a Culture of Rights*. Bangalore: Books for Change for the Centre for Gandhian Studies, Bangalore University.

Kung, Hans, and Karl-Joseph Kuschel (eds.). 1993. *A Global Ethics: The Declaration of the Parliament of the World's Religions*. London: SCM Press.

Macy, Joanna. 1990. The Ecological Self: Postmodern Ground for Right Action. In *Sacred Interconnections: Postmodern Spirituality, Political Economy and Art*, ed. David Ray Griffin, 35–47. Albany: State University of New York Press.

Muzaffar, Chandra. 2005. *Global Ethic or Global Hegemony? Reflections on Religion, Human Dignity and Civilizational Interaction*. London: ASEAN Academic Press.

Rodrigue, Barry, Leonid Grinin, and Andrey Korotayev (eds.). 2017. *From Big Bang to Galactic Civilization: A Big History Anthology*. New Delhi: Primus Books.

Rorty, Richard. 1982. *Consequences of Pragmatism*. Brighton: Harvester Press.

Schieffer, Alexander, and Ronnie Lessem. 2014. *Integral Development: Realizing the Transformative Potential of Individuals, Organizations and Societies*. Farnham and Burlington, VT: Gower.

Todorov, Tzvetan. 2010. *The Fear of Barbarians: Beyond the Clash of Civilizations*. Cambridge: Polity.

Unger, Roberto Mangabeira. 2001. *False Necessity: Anti-necessitarian Social Theory in the Service of Radical Democracy*. London and New York: Verso.

Van Steenbergen, Bart. 1994. Towards a Global, Ecological Citizen. In *The Condition of Citizenship*, ed. Bart van Steenbergen, 14–28. London and Thousand Oaks: Sage.
Wilber, Ken. 2000. *A Theory of Everything: An Integral Vision for Business, Politics, Science and Spirituality*. Boston and London: Shambhala.
Wilson, Edward O. 1982. *On Human Nature*. New York and London: Bantam Books.
Young, Alison. 2005. *Judging the Image: Art, Value, Law*. London and New York: Routledge.

CHAPTER 5

Globalization and the Transnationalisation of Culture: Implications for Cultural Rights

The question of globalization now takes a central place in contemporary intellectual and political economy debates, not only in the social sciences, but also in fields as diverse as literary studies, comparative religion, and art history. This is because of widespread agreement that of all the forces shaping the world today, it is indeed globalization that frames almost every social process, whether they be economic systems, ecological patterns, international relations, media, information technology or the movement of peoples. But while there may be agreement that the globally interconnected nature of these processes has now reached historically unprecedented levels and intensity, there is less agreement about how to conceptualize these planet-wide processes and transformations and their implications. Do they signal the emergence of a benign and united world community, or do they rather represent deepening social and economic inequalities, the domination of the globe by a few powerful actors, and systematic loss of sovereignty and self-determination by both national governments and individuals (Held and McGrew 2003)?

To open this Pandora's box is to let out a host of questions, with new ones constantly emerging as the complexities of contemporary history, ecology and political economy intersect and influence each other in ever changing configurations. Many of these relate directly to culture: the possibility of sustainable cultures in a highly globalized world, the significance or even possibility of "localization" as new counterpart to globalization and the factors that influence the success or failure of social movements that either oppose globalization in general, or which focus

J. Clammer, *Cultural Rights and Justice*,
https://doi.org/10.1007/978-981-13-2811-4_5

on some aspect of it, such as peak-oil or climate change, both being seen as consequences of the hegemonic neo-liberal capitalist world economy (Feola and Nunes 2014). Likewise, issues of citizenship as raised in the previous chapter, of new cosmopolitan identities (Papastergiadis 2012), of "border-crossing", either literally in a geographical sense or conceptually in art, interdisciplinary studies and translation, the emergence of new hybrid forms of culture, and the ethical and practical considerations of appropriation and cultural borrowing in the generation of new forms of cultural expression—in theatre for example (Bharucha 1993).

It is in response to this complexity that a whole suite on conceptual innovations and terminology have emerged—globalization itself, the less formal concept of "internationalization" that was widely used in Japan in the late 1980s and early 1990s, the "World Systems" theory pioneered by Immanuel Wallerstein, the historical model of Ferdinand Braudel, and the notion of "glocalization" popularized by the sociologist Roland Robertson to characterize the interplay between the global and the local, being primary examples. If it is reasonable to say that the early phase of interest in globalization was concerned primarily with the increasing integration of economic systems, it became quickly apparent that cultural and sociological factors are also deeply implicated in and indicative of, planet-wide socioeconomic transformations. Such factors include the international reach of the media, and the recognition of the category of "World Cities" as not only command centers of the world economy, but also as the major spatial locations of the production and dissemination of culture in the form of music, fashion, publishing, film, comics, theatre, television, design and more (Zukin 1995). The extensive contemporary movement of peoples, whether voluntarily for economic or professional reasons, or as tourists, or involuntary as political or environmental refugees, means not only the physical movement of populations, but also the transmission of their cultures and religions (Clammer 2015b, 2018). An empirical result of this has been the increasing hybridization of cultures, and a conceptual one the recognition that cultural processes are a major dimension of globalization (Tomlinson 2000). Out of the relationship between these two dimensions has emerged the concept of transnationalism: the cross-border transmission of intangible elements as well as material ones. Such movement has implications for the protection and preservation of cultural diversity, and it is noteworthy that in its 2005 Convention on the Protection and Promotion of the Diversity of Cultural Expressions specifically singles out the problematic dimensions of globalization as a leading source of the erosion of indigenous cultures and the corresponding spread of global monocultures (UNESCO 2005).

Defining Cultural Transnationalism

The earliest systematic use of the term "transnationalism" was to label multinational business corporations as "Transnational Corporations", or TNCs for short (Grieves 1979), a usage still retained in the literature critical of the forms of globalization identified primarily with the dominance of predatory forms of international capitalism. The term has since then been broadened to also encompass cultural dimensions including film (e.g. Lu 1997), the cultural politics of identity, migration, postcolonial studies, diaspora studies, and those areas of political science and international relations concerned with post-nationalism and the alleged decline of the state in relation to other international actors, whether multilateral institutions or elements of international civil society. This broadening of meaning is important for two reasons. One is to signal the recognition that cultural flows and processes are a significant dimension of globalization (for a set of case studies see Ben-Ari and Clammer 2000). The other is methodological and points to the necessity of a multidisciplinary approach to the study of globalization that must include the internationalization of structures of knowledge production and distribution, the transnationalisation of popular culture (Iwabuchi 2002; Iwabuchi et al. 2004; Kiely and Marfleet 1998), and of religion (Beyer 1997; Clammer 2009). Accompanying or fueling these are migration on a large scale leading to the foundation of diaspora communities in places far from the original ethnic or geographical homelands, and with complex communication and cultural, political and economic networks between them, and the emergence of the ethnically and culturally diverse cities that are now so characteristic of contemporary cultural forms.

A key element in cultural transnationalism is the recognition that in the contemporary world, geographical and social spaces are no longer identical. Melbourne (Australia) is now the second largest Greek city in the world after Athens; Bradford (UK) has a larger Muslim population than many Middle Eastern cities. Almost all major cities in the contemporary world are multiethnic and multicultural, and if the countryside is less so, it nevertheless consumes the hybrid and transnational culture of the metropolis in its television and film viewing, music, reading, the foods in the local store and almost certainly in what its population is wearing. The notion of a "transnational social space" has consequently emerged as an attempt to capture these diverse phenomena, and to situate them within a model of globalization as a totalizing project (Pries 1999).

Modeling Cultural Transnationalism

The study of cultural transnationalism then requires the crossing of traditional disciplinary lines, and also raises questions of cultural representation, ethics, methodology and the dynamics of the emergence of new cultural forms. Transnationality is itself both a structural and a subjective, and raises many interesting sociological issues. Studies have shown for example how economic transactions across borders are frequently based on networks of kinship, personal contacts and trust, often involving largely people of the same ethnic, dialect or caste community. It is migration and the emergence of the Internet and the mobile phone that has provided the fuel for these networks. A focus purely on the national does not allow the nature of these globalized spaces to be grasped, and certainly occludes the subjectivities and autobiographical experiences and projects of people whose life conditions span multiple locales, whether actual physical ones, or "virtual" ones enabled either by information technology or by adherence to a spatially dispersed community such as a particular religion.

Such transnational characteristics apply not only to TNCs, multilateral global institutions, religions and cultural and ethnic networks, but increasingly also to international humanitarian and environmental NGOs, and social movements such as the ecological movement, and, paradoxically, the anti-globalization movement itself. Many of these movements both see their field of action and propaganda as being the globe as a whole, and also intensively utilize the information technology, media and trans-border communication and transportation networks that make such a global reach and action feasible (Keck and Sikkink 1998). This has rightly triggered a major scholarly turn to exploring the key role of information technology in enabling transnational social, cultural and political processes, including such issues as the changing basis of social power and cultural capital, "e-protest", consumption, crime (including new forms of cyber-crime), new forms of mobilization on the part of social movements, and new concepts of citizenship (Webster 2001).

As suggested in the previous chapter, the issue of citizenship has become central to debates about globalization as new notions of global citizenship have emerged (Hudson and Slaughter 2007; Davidson 2004), in large part as a response to the (correct) perception that the large issues that now confront the whole planetary community—such as climate change—are totally trans-border in nature. An aspect of this is the emergence of the idea of *cultural citizenship*—solidarity between peoples based on shared values, religion and cultural projects, rather than on traditional political identities which mean less and less as old-style national sovereignty erodes and as transnational players come to dominate the global stage. Such a situation has major implications for the notion of democracy when the traditional systems of political representation no longer match the globalized reality (Anderson 2002).

The basis, then, of the concept of cultural transnationalism is that empirically a huge number of cross-border *cultural* transactions constantly take place—in the arts, in film, in popular culture—and that many forms of transnational communities do indeed exist (a classic example being the "colleges" of scientific colleagues dispersed globally, but in frequent communication with one another and often collaborating on common projects). The result is that many of the traditional categories of political geography—continents, nations and regions—dissolve in the face of the diasporic and hybrid nature of contemporary transnational interactions (Lewis and Wigen 1997). A new notion of *space* is central to these processes—that social spaces are now disembedded and separate from geographical ones, that there has been a radical global widening of social relations, and that modes of transport and communication have led to a relative annihilation of space, or what David Harvey in a celebrated phrase has called "space-time compression" (Harvey 1989). Space, then, should now be conceptualized in terms of flows rather than as bounded geometry. But as some commentators have rightly noted, such spaces are also often fragmented, and have not only shrunk, but also become transformed in their sociological, subjective and cultural qualities. The dialectic between the global and the local re-emerges at this point, since the "global" is in practice produced and reproduced in specific localities, not in some abstract and unrooted space (Kirsch 1995; Robertson 1994).

This transformation of space is exemplified by the fact that one of the most common usages of the concept of transnationalism is in relation to migration and its sociological and cultural characteristics and consequences. Beginning around 1992 with Glick Schiller, Basch and Blanc-Szanton's study of transmigrants which showed that the social worlds of such migrants are not simply extensions of their communities of origin (although they also retain elements of that), but form new social "fields" reoriented in both space and time, the recognition of the sociological and emotional complexity of migrant's life-worlds has become a dominant perspective. Representative examples would include Leichman's study of Lebanese migrants to French-speaking Africa (Leichman 2005), studies of religious networks among South American migrants to North America, the anthropology of migration in Oceania (Chappell 1999), and analyses of Chinese transnationalism (Louie 2000), as well as more theoretical attempts to grasp such processes in terms of wider concepts of citizenship and culture (Faist 2000; Munch 2001). Certainly these issues have emerged strongly in relation to new political configurations such as the EU (Berezin and Schain 2003). These diverse studies show not only the complex dialectic between the global and the local, but also between indigenous notions of identity and new ones formed out of new subjectivities and social roles that configure the migrant's new life situation (Andolina et al. 2005 for a representative case study).

An emerging issue in migration studies then has not been the actual physical movement of peoples as of the cultural implications of this movement. This involves the migration of artifacts and cultural forms, including music (Connell and Gibson 2004) and art (Clammer 2011a, 2015a), film, fashion and foods, and on the uses of the technology that is making such border crossings so easy—for example the Internet and its role in revitalizing Chinese culture among transnational Chinese migrants (Yang 2003). For this reason, the study of the media has become central to the analysis of diasporic communities and networks since it is evident that access to IT, telecommunications, film and print media makes the formation and continuation of such communities possible (Karim 2003). The notion of culture itself should be read here in a broad sense as not only involving expressive culture and sociological patterns such as gender relations, but also as encompassing such phenomena as transnational accounting, crime, the adoption of children, health and disease patterns, diets, religion and the transformation of the notion of "home" (Al-Ali and Koser 2002). One result of these processes is the formation of "border identities" as permanently "ambiguous" or negotiated identities at the points of intersection of two or more communities (Wilson and Donnan 1998).

Transnationalism and Cultural Studies

It has been a valuable side effect of international migration studies that the analysis of transnationalism has spilt over into cultural studies and informed a whole range of issues including those of ethnicity, identity, hybridity and diaspora, and of course the issues of cultural rights and cultural protection that these involve. A valuable collection of articles that was published when many of these issues were emerging (Vertovec and Cohen 1999) signaled this new configuration very well. Divided into three sections, the contributors discuss in the first the cultural sociology of migration—kinship networks, remittances and cultural citizenship. In the second the concept of diaspora—identity politics, myths of the homeland and the political and social implications of these new forms of multiculturalism. In the third, the notion of transnationalism as "globalization from below", suggesting that globalization is not only brought about by TNCs and neo-liberal capitalism, but also occurs from the bottom up. This occurs through the actual movement of peoples, the transmission of culture and especially popular culture, the creation of new transnational identities and subjectivities, and new forms of interaction between the global and the local (c.f. Smith and Guarnizo 1998).

Among the intellectual fruits of this approach has been the formulation of a new form of political economy in which formerly separated issues—TNCs, ethnicity, multilateral institutions, media, science, law, culture and even linguistics, are brought together in a new and mutually informative configuration which not only illustrates their interdependence, but also the relations of domination that often obtain between them (Hamm and Smandych 2005). This in turn has stimulated the emergence of new concepts of culture, transcending the limitations of the older, bounded, anthropological ones: the recognition of transnational cultures as a distinct category of culture that are not confined to a specific place, class, or ethnic group, but which exist, and indeed are defined by, their ignoring of spatial boundaries (Kennedy and Roudometof 2002). As is noted in several places in this book, the older concept of the "cosmopolitan" which has largely fallen out of academic discourse, has been revived as a term describing the actual experiences or sociopolitical life-worlds of a large number of people for whom flexible or multiple citizenship, participation in several cultural spheres, and a sense of universalism is the norm rather than the exception.

The corresponding range of applications of the idea of cultural nationalism has been great. It has for example revitalized large areas of Asian studies, previously mostly concerned with the "classical" cultures of South, Southeast and East Asia, by introducing such themes as intercultural communication (Wilson and Dissanayake 1996), popular culture, gendered labor migration (entertainers and domestic servants), and the relationships between transnational cultural and sociological developments and new forms of social inequality (Scrase et al. 2003). Other themes include Asian diasporas and their relationship to culture, ethnicity and identity, and Asian cinema. Likewise, it has uncovered ways in which new forms of older cultural practices (teahouses, theatre, fashions and religions) are being reinvented and reinserted into contemporary local, regional and international consumer culture (Iwabuschi et al. 2004). The issue of consumption has itself become central to the understanding of transnational flows (and for contemporary culture in general), since it is as much the movement of artifacts and images as it is the physical movement of peoples that fuels transnationalism, creates transnational consumer cultures, and creates models of identity formation and status seeking, especially for the international upper and middle classes and for the new middle classes of Asia (Crang et al. 2003; Clammer 1997, 2002).

Cultural Transnationalism and Critical Theory

While the transnationalisation of culture is clearly a highly significant part of globalization, we must also bear in mind that globalization is also a highly ideological concept, disputed in its meanings and significance by both its promoters and its detractors. Many of the latter have been willing to risk life and limb by taking to the streets and not only to the printed page or website, as we have seen so clearly in Seattle, Genoa, Hong Kong and other cities where the World Trade Organization and similar bodies have sought to hold their meetings. While there is indeed a celebratory literature on transnationalism, it clearly has its darker underside. Globalization is not only the relatively benign spread of food cultures, music, travel and tourism, fashion and art, but also, primarily through its economic mechanisms, the promoter of many forms of ecological destruction, resource depletion, human exploitation, new forms of inequality and exclusion, family disruption, psychic stress and injustices. While at one level the mobility of labor may be celebrated, at another—the living conditions of migrant workers, inability to communicate with the host society, marginality in relation to cultural and educational opportunities in the new society of residence, the emotional situation of their wives and children accompanying them or left behind in the home country—clearly raise serious issues of concern. The very nature of transnationalism, in throwing up issues of cultural citizenship as well as those of political membership and social inclusion, poses new questions for human rights theory and practice, especially when the original (1948) Universal Declaration of Human Rights is recontextualized in the new situation of globally extended cultures (De Sousa Santos 1999; Cowan et al. 2001). The transnational experience of the highly paid and mobile executive of an international corporation, and that experienced by his Filipina maid or the Thai or South Indian laborer who built his luxury apartment are hardly the same in material rewards, cultural quality, life chances or access to social, political, legal, and medical resources and protections. The experience of transnationalism is as frequently as much one of exile and up-rooting as it is of the enjoyment of the material, cultural and psychological fruits of globalization. Of necessity then, issues of both human and cultural rights are posed in new and complex ways by a new and complex world.

Transnationalism, Methodology and Theory

The concern with cultural transnationalism then certainly requires a rethinking of methodology. "Flows", while not necessarily undermining such traditional concepts as culture, community and region, reconstitutes them in a context of dynamism in which change is not only continuous, but is fed by many intersecting factors, economic, ecological, sociological and technological. This necessitates a move from thinking of "areas" (as in the older "Area Studies" approach) to the study of transnational processes themselves (Mintz 1998). The social sciences in the past, at least until the advent of World Systems theory, tended to make little reference to the larger global structures in which local cultural practices were embedded, but we certainly understand today that it is necessary to explore systematically the connections between culture, transnational movements of people, images and commodities, global capitalism and the activities of both states and non-state actors.

The authors of a significant early paper on these articulations (Szanton Blanc et al. 1995) note that while more and more people are living trans-border lives, capital accumulation is becoming more global and "flexible"—as are labor practices—yet many nation-states are closing their borders to migrants and asylum seekers and to all but the most highly qualified professionals. These complex and ever evolving relationships suggest to the authors a number of theoretical and methodological conclusions, including the necessity for an historical grasp of the forces reconfiguring the shifting relationships between these elements, of a spatial perspective as capitalism deploys itself in different parts of the world, of situating transnational cultural processes and identity politics in the context of states and other regimes of power that seek to regulate economies and discipline people, and an analysis of the relationships between identity and culture on the one hand, and the nature of global capital on the other. That particular year seems to have been a fruitful one in initiating new approaches to a globalized world, seeing also the publication of suggestive new models of the relationships between culture and capitalism, and of the structures that mediate between them including the media, tourism, and consumption practices (Kearney 1995), and the recognition of the need for multi-sited ethnography, since the activity of transnational culture lies in the flows themselves as well as in the points of transmission and reception (Marcus 1995). In a situation where large numbers of people now live outside of their traditional national, political and social boundaries, important questions about reformulating conceptions of human and cultural rights arise (Kemp et al. 2011).

Zygmunt Bauman has argued at some length (Bauman 2000, 2004) that the processes of modernity unmoor people from their original socio-cultural settings and sets them adrift in what he calls "liquid modernity" in which not only are notions of time and space, work and self, individuality and the other, transformed and disrupted, but also that the human costs of such radical upheavals are often high, generating at their worst "human waste"—outcasts drifting the world with few roots and fewer prospects. These processes are not even totally new—hence the need for a historical grasp of the forces that have created and shaped modernity. As A.G. Frank has ably demonstrated, globalization itself is not new, but has its roots in patterns of trade and migration of considerable antiquity (Frank 1998).

While older models of globalization and transnationalism tended to focus on economic relationships and physical migration, we now see clearly that it is necessary to create new models based equally on what Lash and Urry aptly called "Economies of Signs and Space (Lash and Urry 1994). That is to say that globalization itself now takes place largely through cultural mechanisms—the spread of images through film, television, advertising, the international art market, and the migration of "cultural creatives"—writers, artists, fashion designers, musicians, media people, internationally mobile academics, architects—who live transnational lives and carry their image universes with them as they move and travel. The spread of modernism in art, architecture, design and literature is an earlier example of this process in action. German architects such as Mies van der Rohe and Walter Gropius carried the idea of the "international style" from continental Europe to the United States, from whence it diffused even further. Their former Bauhaus colleagues in design (Laszlo Moholy-Nagy), painting (Joseph Albers), textiles (Anni Albers), furniture design (Marcel Breuer) and others carried European artistic and design ideas to north and south America, to England, and as far as India (Clammer 2011b). The process now continues through cinema, popular culture, sport, tourism, publications, the World Wide Web and many other cultural mechanisms (Appadurai 1996).

Transnationalism and Cultural Rights

Space has always been politicized—concerns with mapping, territories, borders, sovereignty, still dominate a good deal of political discourse and practice. But lines on a map and the actual movement of peoples and their cultures are altogether different things. In a world in which the old boundaries mean, for a very large number of people, something quite different from what they did a generation or two ago, a rethinking of the new transnational processes in relation to development and to cultural rights is necessary. For example, a concept of "culture and development" that does not take into account that "cultures" are now radically different entities or sets of processes from how they were conceived in the less globalized past, cannot possibly grapple with the relationship between the two, or conceive that the relationship itself is now very different. A great deal of development thinking is now turning to the idea not of culture *and* development, but rather the development *of* culture—the stimulation of "cultural industries" and of the economic and poverty alleviation possibilities inherent in the visual and performative arts and crafts of "developing" societies (UNESCO and UNDP 2013;

Clammer 2015b). Such an idea has many implications—for cultural policy (often itself weak or missing), for stimulating empowerment and cultural self-confidence that arises from the recognition that one's cultural productions are valued and consumed, perhaps well beyond one's own national or regional boundaries, and for the very preservation and protection of cultural diversity which UNESCO itself promotes.

Such considerations immediately implicate cultural rights in a number of ways. The first is the point essentially made above—that a transnational culture requires a transnational conception of cultural rights. The existing UNESCO understanding of culture seems to be still a relatively static and even essentialist one. Transnationalism however overthrows such any such notion. While relatively bounded cultures certainly do exist (although the word "relatively" is crucial here), many contemporary cultural expressions are much less so, if at all. The implication of this is clearly that the "preservation and protection" of cultural expressions already means the preservation and protection of hybrid, transnational and geographically unrooted forms of culture. While the 2005 UNESCO Convention seeks to protect cultures from the dangers of globalization, it is in reality this very globalization that is creating new forms of culture. Any contemporary notion of cultural rights must thus itself be a "transnational" one, one recognizing and affirming the fluid and ever shifting nature of cultural expressions. A better model for this world might well be Chaos Theory rather than conventional social-structural approaches to social life, one in which "disorder" is normal, but in which "strange attractors" exist which allow apparently chaotic phenomena to group themselves in coherent patterns, or, in this context, what we think of as "cultures".

A second implication, as also noted above, is that the relationship between "culture" and "development" also radically changes. Not only is culture itself reformulated in process and transnational terms, but development itself is seen anew as a cultural project, rather than a purely economic or political one. The emphasis in so much recent thought and practice in social movements and elsewhere on such issues as identity politics, sexuality and gender issues, race, rights of free-speech, ecology, religious freedom, multiculturalism, removal of censorship and so forth, clearly signals the way in which cultural issues have taken a central place in debates about cultural futures, social justice and human rights. This suggests a new role for cultural policy. Many countries lack any coherent cultural policy, and when they do have one it is rarely directed towards any kind of development goals. The Sustainable Development Goals announced by the United Nations, while laudable in themselves, are likely to be ineffective unless they are expanded to include the absent dimension of culture, and unless culture is seen as the vehicle through which many of the goals might be best attained.

While the fundamental notion of rights may indeed be universal, their contextualization is vital. In a world now irreversibly globalized, at least in the near future (after "peak oil" who knows?) both cultures and their rights to exist and flourish need reconceptualizing, and appropriate legal and policy instruments enacted to ensure their protection. Here we come back to a principle enunciated elsewhere in this book: that cultural diversity is as important as bio-diversity and that, in fact, the two support each other. This principle I still hold to be true: the expanded context however is that in a situation of transnational cultures as being now a normal phenomenon, cultural rights themselves must be understood in this fluid context, or what might be expressed as the right to hybridity, the right to be cosmopolitan, and the celebration of the fact that we all now have access to cultural expressions once remote or inaccessible, or simply unknown to many of us. This is not to dilute the significance of cultural rights, but rather to embark on the adventure of reasserting them, in new forms perhaps, in the contemporary transnational context.

References

Al-Ali, Nadje, and Khalid Koser (eds.). 2002. *New Approaches to Migration? Transnational Communities and the Transformation of Home*. London and New York: Routledge.

Anderson, James (ed.). 2002. *Transnational Democracy: Political Spaces and Border Crossings*. London and New York: Routledge.

Andolina, Robert, Sarah Radcliffe, and Nina Laurie. 2005. Development and Culture: Transnational Identity Making in Bolivia. *Political Geography* 24 (6): 678–702.

Appadurai, Arjun. 1996. *Modernity at Large: Cultural Dimensions of Globalization*. Minneapolis: University of Minnesota Press.

Bauman, Zygmunt. 2000. *Liquid Modernity*. Cambridge: Polity Press.

Bauman, Zygmunt. 2004. *Wasted Lives: Modernity and Its Outcasts*. Cambridge: Polity Press.

Ben-Ari, Eyal, and John Clammer (eds.). 2000. *Japan in Singapore: Cultural Occurances and Cultural Flows*. Richmond: Curzon Press.

Berezin, Mabel, and Martin Schain. 2003. *Europe Without Borders: Remapping Territory, Citizenship and Identity in a Transnational Age*. Baltimore: Johns Hopkins University Press.
Beyer, Peter. 1997. *Religion and Globalization*. London and Thousand Oaks: Sage.
Bharucha, Rustom. 1993. *Theatre and the World: Performance and the Politics of Culture*. London and New York: Routledge.
Chappell, D.A. 1999. Transnationalism in Central Oceanian Politics: A Dialectic of Diasporas and Nationhood. *Journal of the Polynesian Society* 108 (3): 277–303.
Clammer, John. 1997. *Contemporary Urban Japan: A Sociology of Consumption*. Oxford and Malden, MA : Blackwell.
Clammer, John. 2002. *Diaspora and Identity: The Sociology of Culture in Southeast Asia*. Petaling Jaya and London: Pelanduk Publications and ASEAN Academic Press.
Clammer, John. 2009. *Diaspora and Belief: Globalisation, Religion and Identity in Postcolonial Asia*. New Delhi: Shipra Publications.
Clammer, John. 2011a. Art and the Conception and Creation of 'Asia': Towards a New Model of Social Theory. *Asia Pacific World* 2 (1): 5–24.
Clammer, John. 2011b. Bauhaus in Asia: Future Model or Modernist Past? In *Bauhaus and the City: A Contested Heritage for a Challenging Future*, ed. Laura Colini and Frank Eckardt, 113–128. Wurzburg: Konigshausen and Neuman (Bauhaus Urban Studies 1).
Clammer, John. 2015a. Migrating Artists/Migrating Art: Intra-Asian Movement, New Asian Arts and New Sociologies of Artistic Consumption and Education. In *Global Art and Diasporic Art in Japan and Asia*, Mori Art Museum, 246–256. Tokyo: Mori Art Museum, MAM Documents 002 (in Japanese).
Clammer, John. 2015b. *Art, Culture and International Development: Humanizing Social Transformation*. London and New York: Routledge.
Clammer, John. 2018. Dialogue Through the Image: Asian Christian Art and Inter-religious Discourses in Historical and Contemporary Asia. *International Journal of Asian Christianity* 1 (1): 117–133.
Connell, J., and C. Gibson. 2004. World Music: Deterritorializing Place and Identity. *Progress in Human Geography* 28 (3): 342–361.
Cowan, Jane, Marie-Benedicte Dembour, and Richard A. Wilson (eds.). 2001. *Culture and Rights: Anthropological Perspectives*. Cambridge: Cambridge University Press.
Crang, P., C. Dwyer, and P. Jackson. 2003. Transnationalism and the Spaces of Commodity Culture. *Progress in Physical Geography* 27 (4): 438–456.
Davidson, Julie. 2004. Citizenship and Sustainability: Rights and Responsibilities in the Global Age. In *Controversies in Environmental Sociology*, ed. Rob White, 168–184. Cambridge: Cambridge University Press.

De Sousa Santos, Boaventura. 1999. Towards a Multicultural Conception of Human Rights. In *Spaces of Culture*, ed. Mike Featherstone and Scott Lash, 214–229. London and Thousand Oaks: Sage.

Faist, T. 2000. Transnationalization in International Migration: Implications for the Study of Citizenship and Culture. *Ethnic and Racial Studies* 23 (2): 189–222.

Feola, Giuseppe, and Richard Nunes. 2014. Success and Failure of Grassroots Innovations for Addressing Climate Change: The Case of the Transition Movement. *Global Environmental Change* 24: 232–250.

Frank, Andre Gunder. 1998. *ReOrient: Global Economy in the Asian Age*. Berkeley and London: University of California Press.

Glick Schiller, N., Linda Basch, and Cristina Blanc-Szanton (eds.). 1992. *Towards a Transnational Perspective on Migration: Race, Class, Ethnicity and Nationalism Reconsidered*. New York: Academy of Social Sciences.

Grieves, Forest L. 1979. *Transnationalism in World Politics and Business*. New York: Pergamon Press.

Hamm, Bernd, and Russell Smandych (eds.). 2005. *Cultural Imperialism: Essays on the Political Economy of Cultural Domination*. Peterborough, ON: Broadview Press.

Harvey, David. 1989. *The Condition of Postmodernity*. Oxford: Blackwell.

Held, David, and Anthony McGrew (eds.). 2003. *The Global Transformations Reader: An Introduction to the Globalization Debate*. Cambridge: Polity Press.

Hudson, Wayne, and Steven Slaughter (eds.). 2007. *Globalization and Citizenship: The Transnational Challenge*. London and New York: Routledge.

Iwabuchi, Koichi. 2002. *Recentering Globalization: Popular Culture and Japanese Transnationalism*. Durham, NC and London: Duke University Press.

Iwabuchi, Koichi, Stephen Muecke, and Mandy Thomas (eds.). 2004. *Rogue Flows: Trans-Asian Cultural Traffic*. Hong Kong: Hong Kong University Press.

Karim, Karim H. (ed.). 2003. *The Media of Diaspora*. London and New York: Routledge (Routledge Research on Transnationalism, 7).

Kearney, M. 1995. The Local and the Global: The Anthropology of Globalization and Transnationalism. *Annual Review of Anthropology* 24: 547–565.

Keck, Margaret E., and Kathryn Sikkink. 1998. *Activists Beyond Borders: Advocacy Networks in International Politics*. Ithaca: Cornell University Press.

Kemp, Walter, Vesselin Popovski, and Ramesh Thakur (eds.). 2011. *Blood and Borders: The Responsibility to Protect and the Problem of the Kin-State*. Tokyo, Paris and New York: United Nations University Press.

Kennedy, Paul, and Victor Roudometof (eds.). 2002. *Communities Across Borders: New Immigrants and Transnational Cultures*. New York and London: Routledge.

Kiely, Ray, and Phil Marfleet (eds.). 1998. *Globalization and the Third World*. London and New York: Routledge.
Kirsch, Scott. 1995. The Incredible Shrinking World? Technology and the Production of Space. *Environment and Planning D: Society and Space* 13: 529–555.
Lash, Scott, and John Urry. 1994. *Economies of Signs and Space*. London: Sage.
Leichman, M.A. 2005. The Legacy of Transnational Lives: Beyond the First Generation of Lebanese in Senegal. *Ethnic and Racial Studies* 28 (4): 663–686.
Lewis, Martin W., and Karen E. Wigen. 1997. *The Myth of Continents: A Critique of Metageography*. Berkeley and London: University of California Press.
Louie, A. 2000. Re-territorializing Transnationalism: Chinese Americans and the Chinese Motherland. *American Ethnologist* 27 (3): 645–669.
Lu, Sheldon Hsiao-peng (ed.). 1997. *Transnational Chinese Cinema: Identity, Nationhood, Gender*. Honolulu: University of Hawai'i Press.
Marcus, George E. 1995. Ethnography in/of the World System: The Emergence of Multi-sited Ethnography. *Annual Review of Anthropology* 24: 95–117.
Mintz, S.W. 1998. The Localization of Anthropological Practice: From Area Studies to Transnationalism. *Critique of Anthropology* 18 (2): 117–133.
Munch, Richard. 2001. *Nation and Citizenship in the Global Age: from National to Transnational Ties and Identities*. New York: Palgrave.
Papastergiadis, Nikos. 2012. *Cosmopolitanism and Culture*. Cambridge and Malden, MA: Polity Press.
Pries, Ludger (ed.). 1999. *Migration and Transnational Social Spaces*. Aldershot: Ashgate.
Robertson, Roland. 1994. Glocalization: Space, Time and Social Theory. *Journal of International Communication* 1 (1): 4–20.
Scrase, Timothy J., T.J.M. Holden, and Scott Baum (eds.). 2003. *Globalization and Inequality in Asia*. Melbourne: Trans Pacific Press.
Smith, Michael P., and Luis Eduardo Guarnizo (eds.). 1998. *Transnationalism from Below*. New Brunswick, NJ: Transaction Publishers.
Szanton Blanc, Cristina, Linda Basch, and Nina Glick Schiller. 1995. Transnationalism, Nation-States and Culture. *Current Anthropology* 36 (4): 683–686.
Tomlinson, John. 2000. *Globalization and Culture*. Cambridge: Polity Press.
UNESCO. 2005. *Convention on the Protection and Promotion of the Diversity of Cultural Expressions*. Paris: UNESCO.
UNESCO and UNDP. 2013. *Creative Economy Report 2013: Widening Local Development Pathways*. Paris and New York: UNESCO and UNDP.
Vertovec, Steven, and Robin Cohen (eds.). 1999. *Migration, Diasporas and Transnationalism*. Cheltenham and Northampton, MA: Edward Elgar.

Webster, Frank (ed.). 2001. *Culture and Politics in the Information Age: A New Politics?* New York and London: Routledge.

Wilson, Rob, and Wimal Dissanayake (eds.). 1996. *Global/Local: Cultural Production and Transnational Imagery.* Durham, NC and London: Duke University Press.

Wilson, Thomas, and Hastings Donnan (eds.). 1998. *Border Identities.* Cambridge and New York: Cambridge University Press.

Yang, G.B. 2003. The Internet and the Rise of the Transnational Chinese Sphere. *Media, Culture and Society* 25 (4): 469–499.

Zukin, Sharon. 1995. *The Cultures of Cities.* Oxford: Blackwell.

CHAPTER 6

Visual Justice: The Right to Beauty?

Does, or should cultural justice include visual justice—the right not to be exposed to ugliness and the visual pollution so characteristic of much of contemporary society, its architecture and its landscapes, and the corresponding right to be exposed to beauty—to harmonious and pleasing visual (and perhaps aural) environments that produce sensations of pleasure and that distinctive but unclassifiable feeling that comes with pristine natural environments and great art and music? Certainly no list of human rights known to me includes the right to beauty, but at the same time, the older lists of human needs invariably include aesthetic needs among the elements needed for a satisfactory human life. This chapter will argue that the right to beauty (a category naturally understood differently in different cultures) is indeed a cultural right, and one that should be pursued through cultural activism, art movements and eco-criticism. I certainly include the latter in the light of the mounting evidence, embodied in the relatively new field of environmental psychology, that exposure to natural beauty is an essential requirement for a rounded human life, and is a major source of both psychic and physical healing. The expanding field of environmental aesthetics likewise suggests a close link between attractive environments and cultural satisfaction, including such initially unlikely aspects as decreased depression, crime and health therapies, whether based primarily in art or in nature. It can also be cogently argued that there are many links between visual justice and sustainability, mediated by a number of factors including the desire to create or maintain attractive environments, good design and architecture

J. Clammer, *Cultural Rights and Justice*,
https://doi.org/10.1007/978-981-13-2811-4_6

(on eco-psychology see Roszak et al. 1995; on environmental aesthetics, from a growing literature see Brady 2003; Budd 2005; on art, design and sustainability Clammer 2015: 39–62).

The notion of aesthetics then need not be confined only to the realm of art: it has much wider implications, including some very 'applied' ones—ones which flow back into planning, cultural and social policy and development decisions. Any attractive social future implies and requires an attractive environment, both in terms of natural ones, and humanly designed ones, such as cities and individual buildings. Arguments for beauty have been advanced along a number of lines: that beauty is an evolutionary necessity and is not only an intrinsic part of any flourishing culture, but is required for its survival (for example by Dutton 2010; Rothenberg 2011), that any future society, including a socialist and post-capitalist one, will require art as part of its cultural make-up (Fischer 2010), that beauty is a requirement for social justice (Scarry 2000), that it is intimately connected to the achievement of peace (Lederach 2005) or that the arts, as the embodiment of beauty, are major tools for the teaching of virtue and moral standards (Nussbaum 1995, 2012). I, too, have argued at length for enhancing the connections between the arts and development with the goal of creating holistic and humanizing forms of social transformation (Clammer 2015), and furthermore, that not only are social movements as usually understood by sociologists, actually cultural movements as well, but that art is not an epiphenomenon of society, but one of its generative aspects (Clammer 2014).

But let us, before going further, examine the arguments for the necessity of beauty. These fall into several fairly distinct categories. The first category includes those books arguing for the evolutionary necessity of beauty and its embodiment not only in perceptions and evaluations of natural environments, but in a whole range of cultural practices of art, decoration, design and personal enhancement mostly found among humans, but also shared with other species. Two examples of this genre are the volume by David Rothenberg *Survival of the Beautiful: Art, Science and Evolution* (2011), and the one by Denis Dutton *The Art Instinct: Beauty, Pleasure and Human Evolution* (2009). Both share the common thread that they argue that beauty is not simply a cultural epiphenomenon—nice but not essential to human survival (and that of a number of other species such as the Bowerbird and the male Peacock)—but is fundamental to our evolutionary progress and success. Art, as the most conspicuous manifestation of the deliberate seeking for or desire to produce beauty, is universal because it fulfills this evolutionary role. This is because it is the vehicle of imaginative expression—a key quality of being human—and also, as Dutton argues, allows for the vicarious exploration of reality and its manipulation in various experimental ways. This faculty of imagination raises us above our 'animal' selves and is a major force in what Dutton calls the "self-domestication" of the human species, or perhaps what in another context Norbert Elias called "the civilizing process" (Elias 1978). If there is indeed an "art instinct", then the pursuit of beauty is not a secondary human activity (compared say with economic activity), but fulfills an essential evolutionary function. Certainly both Dutton and Rothenberg make a strong case for such a position, one that has significant implications for politics, sociology and cultural policy.

Somewhat different although with many overlapping concerns is the work of John Armstrong (2005), who, while he does not locate beauty in an evolutionary framework, does argue that it is not only intimately connected with the pursuit of happiness, but is a *need* for the human mind. There are many reasons for this—the innate attraction to proportion, harmony, unity and symmetry, the idea derived from Plotinus that physical beauty points to something beyond itself, and specifically to the image of our soul made perfect, and a certain rather Japanese view of aesthetics that the love of beauty involves yearning for what is not, and maybe cannot be, fulfilled. As Armstrong puts it "For at the core of beauty is a conception of how we would like life to be and yet we know that life cannot be that way" (2005: 85). Paradoxically it is precisely that life is difficult and in a sense "incomplete" that we need beauty—while in itself it represents the perfect, it arises out of imperfection. Hence the human propensity to imagine paradises and to invent utopias. Drawing on both Pierre Boudieu and John Berger however, Armstrong also warns against the dangers of a "politics of taste"—the situation in which a set of values, in this case aesthetic ones is established such that the taste of the dominant class always comes out on top, so that, in Berger's terms, "taste" may be a way of constructing a particularly subtle instrument of exclusion and cultural denigration. But the ideal situation is one in which "The experience of beauty, we may then say, consists in finding spiritual value (truth, happiness, moral ideals) at home in a material setting (rhythm, line, shape, structure) in such a way that, while we contemplate the object, the two seem inseparable" (Armstrong 2005: 163). Beauty then can be said to be fundamental to culture and the development of both the mind and of moral sensibilities, it is both a need and an evolutionary necessity.

A second category, most fully represented by the work of the Marxist thinker Ernst Fischer (2010) and to some extent by his friend, the major critic John Berger (1977) that, while a great deal of art reflects class interests and much or most of the so-called art world is simply conspicuous consumption on a grand scale, that has far more to do with money, status and the commodification of art than with aesthetics, in a future, post-capitalist, society, art will still have a major, but now authentic place. Its expressive qualities, ability to produce beauty in a range of media (visual art, film, dance, theatre, mime and other forms), and its embodiment of deep human needs and search for meaning, will not only continue, but will be supported and enhanced in a genuinely socialist society in which equality and not hierarchies of status will prevail (ideally). The work of the peace scholar and activist John Paul Lederach falls into a category of its own, with its argument that peacebuilding is itself an art form, and that in building peace both the arts and appreciation of nature are intimately involved (Lederach 2005).

But of even more significance to issues of cultural rights are those writers who have argued directly for a connection between beauty and social justice, and it is to these that we will now turn. Here I will concentrate on the developed argument of Elaine Scarry in her important book *On Beauty and Being Just* (Scarry 2000). While many points of her thesis are contestable, the fundamental link that she finds between beauty and justice is highly significant for the position being developed here in relation to cultural rights. Her starting point is the claim that beauty prompts in us the desire to copy it: "the requirement beauty places on us to replicate" (p. 5). This emerges from a view of beauty derived from a range of classical thinkers of antiquity and since—Plato, Homer, Aquinas, Augustine, Dante and Proust—that beauty is "life-saving" (Homer), "life-creating" (Dante) and "life-altering" (Rilke), that it makes life more vivid and animated, and is a form of "greeting": "It lifts away from the neutral background as though coming forward to welcome you – as though the object were designed to 'fit' your perception" (p. 25). Scarry's conception of beauty is thus not a passive one, or one that simply looks back to classical models, important as these are, but is dynamic and has what she calls a "forward momentum" (p. 46)—inciting a desire to bring new things into existence and requiring us to break new ground. Beauty, as Kant noted long ago, is not like other pleasures, but is inexhaustible. Given these characteristics of beauty, Scarry wishes to bring it back into contemporary discourse, from which she believes it has been banished, especially in the humanities.

To do this she feels it necessary to combat what she sees as the main political argument against consideration of beauty, notably that by preoccupying our attention it distracts attention from other, much more pressing, social issues (p. 58). This she counters by arguing that attention to beauty "actually assists us in the work of addressing injustice, not only by requiring us of constant perceptual acuity – high dives of seeing, hearing, touching", but also by increasing our standards of care by extending the consequences of such recognition to other objects and makes us want to protect beautiful things (p. 62). When this is the case "Beauty assists us in our attention to justice" (p. 86), and has other beneficial side-effects including leading to an enhancement of a positive sense of self, produces pleasure, establishes a relationship between rhythm, harmony and justice and encourages us to create beauty that does not yet exist as well as perpetuating beauty that already exists. While I have my doubts about the alleged relationship between symmetry and justice and her belief that one encourages the other, the basic thrust of Scarry's argument is very important in that, far from banishing the idea of beauty to a purely aesthetic category with little social or political import, she rescues it from this limbo and relocates it as a major aspect of social discourse, the pursuit of justice and the physical improvement of the world. It is for exactly these reasons that I argue here for beauty as a right: visual (or auditory, olfactory or sensuous) justice is a significant dimension of the field of justice as a whole.

Scarry herself asserts that "beauty is a starting point for justice" (p. 31), and as John Armstrong also suggests, following Schiller, that is beauty is an "aesthetic necessity" then the "education of the eye" is a vital part of the total educational process (Armstrong 2005: 129), and one much neglected in many educational systems, even those concerned with the liberation of the human subject. In an earlier book, Martha Nussbaum makes a similar point—that literature is central to culture because it not only potentially exposes us to beauty (in good poetry for example), but also expands our imaginative capacities so that we are better equipped to make those judgments that public life demands of us (Nussbaum 1995), and other writers have argued similarly not only for public judgment, but for the expansion of a moral sense and our ethical universe in general (Palmer 1992; Bermudez and Gardner 2003).

Cultural rights and the sense of, access to and ability to freely express beauty are thus intimately related.

The role of the arts as (ideally) carriers of beauty is consequently paramount in relation to holistic development, not least because it has an anticipatory function. As Jacques Ranciere puts it speaking of the role of the arts and aesthetics in general: "If the concept of the avant-garde has any meaning in the aesthetic regime of the arts, it is on this side of things, not on the side of advanced detachments of artistic innovation but on the side of the invention of sensible forms and material structures for a life to come" (Ranciere 2004: 24). Art shapes this "sensible order"—by formulating new forms of subjectivity and making it possible to think the real through fictionalized means. Although the aestheticization of politics has its dangers, as attested historically by its association with the rise of fascism in Europe, any truly radical emancipatory politics requires an aesthetic dimension: without it, any future politics and society are one dimensional and banal. The search for cultural justice is thus radically emancipatory in two senses—it creates the imaginative structures and content of the future society, and it proposes a "non-political" (in the conventional sense) route to such social transformation, one that exists beyond the preoccupation with power that distorts most political discourse and revolutionary practice (Holloway 2002; Clammer 2009).

This is certainly not a new idea—it was argued persuasively by Herbert Marcuse a generation ago (Marcuse 1978, and for an insightful commentary see Becker 1994). For Marcuse repression would stimulate images of liberation, the creative process stimulates resistance. While in a media-saturated society images can all too easily be taken captive by advertising and forms of popular culture and political and social ideologies, nevertheless they possess both subversive and transformative power. Given that society and culture are largely constituted by their symbolic processes and formations, this is necessarily so. The "function" of art then goes well beyond its decorative and entertainment roles to strike deep into the unconscious and to provide the primary vehicle through which the imagination can manifest itself in material forms. It is a space of freedom in a world in which consciousness is constantly colonized by what is effective propaganda, much of it "cultural" in nature (as opposed to overtly political). Marcuse, however, seems to have argued that there is something beyond the "reality principle"—notably the free sphere of the imagination. Here I would differ from him in two respects—the ever present danger of the colonization of the imagination of elements of unfreedom, and the idea that the imagination (and hence art as its vehicle) is not "reality". Given that much of what we take to be reality is in fact socially and culturally constructed, there is often no good reason to suppose that the world that is so often presented to us as "real" is any more so than the products of the imagination out of which most of it arose in the first place.

Nevertheless, Marcuse presents a powerful argument in favor of the idea that the arts reflect true humanness, the site of emotional play and of the exercise of the imaginative faculties that define our species being as much as does work, and indeed artistic production or practice may be seen as an unalienated form of work that merges with what is often seen as the opposite of work—notably play. The literal play—as in the dramas of Bertolt Brecht, especially in his so-called learning plays show this principle at work—theatre that simultaneously comprises performance, social critique, high aesthetic qualities, the expression of the emotions, and hopefully, from the perspective of the audience, both learning and enjoyment. The beautiful for Marcuse is not simply a category of bourgeois aesthetics, but is subversive: it forces us to reconsider nature and culture and to question why both so often, as the result of human agency, deviate so much from the ideal forms that they could take. The sensuous, as Marcuse argued and as I examine in Chapter 10, is often excluded or ignored as a significant aspect of society and culture by progressive movements, when in fact it is at the heart of human relationships to the world, including of course relationships with other humans. The artist therefore has a potentially highly progressive role, and indeed a great responsibility as a prominent cadre of cultural workers not to produce the trivial, but, as the performance artist Guillermo Gomez-Pena puts it "The job of the artist is to force open the matrix of reality to admit unsuspected possibilities" (1994: 212).

In a more recent work Antonio Negri has taken up not so-dissimilar themes (Negri 2012) in a book, taking the form of a series of letters, that discusses the problem of perceiving a world beyond the apparent hegemony of capitalism in which "The society around me seemed like an enormous piling up of commodities, a piling up of abstract values which money and the mechanisms of the financial world were rendering interchangeable" (p. vii) and the possibility of both the production of beauty and of a new conception of labor in, or beyond, such a world. To realize this possibility requires an aesthetics of resistance and demystification, the creation of alternatives within the "given" world, the promotion of the imagination, the recognition that art is the mechanism for the construction of a new "language" with which to critique and reframe reality, and a way of conceiving of forms of labor which are not measured by the criteria of the "productivist" model of work and its vocabulary ("efficiency", "productivity", "growth", "progress"). But while this powerful argument for not just the necessity of art, but for new forms of art beyond the commoditized categories of capitalism, has many parallels with the earlier work of Marcuse, and the arguments being advanced in this book, Negri adds an important additional ingredient, notably the necessity of creating a "passage to ethics, and therefore true potentiality [*Potenza*] of constructing a meaningful world" (p. 29). In the section of the book on "immaterial labor" he expands this idea by suggesting that "In reality, the aesthetic act…ends by finding ethical decision on its path. We are living in a phase of transformation, in which this metamorphosis of space and time which the contemporary accumulation of labor and culture have determined. Within this process of transformation, bodies are stretched. There is a continued presence of crises without "external" solution: we are *here*, and we cannot escape to *elsewhere*. And yet there is this extraordinary spoken word [*parola*] which we know how to express, this creative capacity which we know how to propose. And, because it comprises both the productive and the ontological, the event and the common, art should give ethical meaning to these complex knots, in other words it should help us to construct this multiple paradigm in which being-for-the-other – *qua* being-in-common – triumphs" (Negri 2012: 119–120).

Art and Social Transformation

Such an approach has at least two important implications. On the one hand it ascribes to the arts a major role in social and cultural transformation, and implies a new model that greatly subverts conventional models of political processes, one indeed led by culture rather than culture being a by-product of political change. But culture of course does not stand apart from other social processes, and in particular the economic, something that requires the "culturalization of the economy" rather than the more common process of the colonization of culture by economics. This is a considerable challenge and one that cultural rights activists need to take up vigorously, and to connect it to movements proposing radical alternatives to the dominant neo-liberal paradigm such as many forms of ecological economics, solidarity economy, "post-development" models, localization movements and yet other forms. The other hand requires a rethinking of artistic production and consumption, and a return to debates about the social responsibility of the artist. This is of course a fraught question, since many would argue a contemporary version of the "art for art's sake" position and would suggest that "socially responsible" art would quickly degenerate into the banalities of the kinds of Socialist Realism that at one time dominated artistic production in Soviet Russia and China. But counterarguments to this can easily be found—either empirical ones such as the vibrant poster art produced in socialist Cuba (Cushing 2003), or in the views of practicing artists in various fields themselves. Take for example the statement by the Palestinian writer Abu Haled that "The writer in our times must integrate all forms of writing. There is no pure literature. If the writer cuts himself off from the suffering and the problems of society, this in itself is a form of engagement, but in the cause of evil, in the cause of injustice and oppression. This has nothing to do with Marxist theory. It has to do with the simplest thing in the world: honesty, responsibility. Look, if a painter sits painting the landscape and a small child is murdered in the very field he is painting – if the painter sits and waits until it is over and then resumes painting, he himself is party to the murder!" (Oz 1983: 172). The Indian novelist Amitav Ghosh has recently made the same point much in relation to climate change which he sees as the big issue of the present moment, yet to which few novelists or creative writers have turned, creating a giant silence, a space which imaginative writers should be filling with all their powers (Ghosh 2016).

But while a more obviously "radical" approach can be taken, there are other, more subtle, ones, and here I will take just two examples—the somewhat parallel arguments of Grant Kester and those of Nikos Papastergiadis. In his significant book on collaborative contemporary art (Kester 2011) Kester begins with the observation that as the old narratives lose their legitimacy, space is opened for new stories, new visions and new visions of the future, among which is a deconstruction of the now rather tired concept of "development". In so doing, a number of intriguing proposals arise—for example the idea that engaging in social action may not only be a means to an already defined end, but may in itself transform subjectivity or produce its own forms of unexpected insight (p. 59), or that, for art to be a meaningful vehicle of social change, it is necessary to rethink radically what is meant by "productive labor" (p. 76), since in the view of much of mainstream society, artistic productivity is not really "work" at all, but something closer to play, something inevitably classified as non-work by definition. The problem here then may not be with the activity, but with the definition. Craft for example Kester defines as a kind of "social architecture" in which labor is often cooperative and of a quite different nature from standard wage-labor (p. 90). The body of his book extends this idea to an examination of a range of cooperative and collaborative contemporary art projects or networks in Argentina, India, Senegal, and elsewhere, contradicting the idea of art production as totally individualistic and inward-looking, suggesting an alternative reading of art history. For as Kester summarizes the argument "The history of modern art can be viewed, in large measure, as an ongoing struggle to develop a compensatory cultural response to the destructive and dehumanizing effects of modernity, whether this is done through the agency of a well-crafted object, painting of bucolic Polynesians, or the therapeutic disruption of the viewer's perception" (p. 21). In Kester's view then, art again is a necessary component in the composition of culture for a number of reasons, including that it is perhaps the only element other than critical social theory that actively struggles against the negative consequences of modernity, and that it redefines the nature of work, suggesting that productivity can also be found in what appear to be non-utilitarian forms of activity outside of the usual labor relations and possibly outside of the "market" too. In fact when art gets drawn into the market another set of problems arise, including its commoditization and all of the issues commonly studied by some branches of the sociology of the arts—the gallery system, reputations, prices, competitions and the growing international network of biennales and international art shows. The role of critics and non-artist writers about art, and all the paraphernalia of the "art world". Kester shows, among other things, that there is also an "art world" at least partially outside of those largely commercial networks, one based on cooperation and collective endeavors and addressing contemporary social problems in creative, and fully artistic, ways.

A parallel position is taken by Nikos Papastergiadis in his book *Cosmopolitanism and Culture* (2012) in which he examines a range of art projects in the interests of solidarity, anti-racism, and for the radical and humane reform of refugee and immigration regimes, and against the culture of fear and repression that has grown rapidly since 2011. Papastergiadis is himself, as well as through the medium of the projects that he examines, proposing new forms of political debate that resist dogma, while accepting and illuminating the complexity of the real world situation, and does so by suggesting alternative models of and for cross-cultural dialogue through the arts, and which accept and use creatively the new communication technologies rather than resisting them. This opening up of new "conversations" involves imaginative engagement with the "Other", through the formulation of what Papastergiadis calls "aesthetic cosmopolitanism", which is "evident in a range of locally grounded and globally oriented artistic tendencies – denationalization, reflexive hospitality, cultural translation, discursivity and the global public sphere" (p. 9). This is achieved through "Ethical relations with the other, political networks for activating social change, and cultural platforms for facilitating change [that] have become powerful themes that have informed the practice of many contemporary artists. This fascination with the nexus between art and politics has inspired me to propose that artists are knowledge partners in the theories of cosmopolitanism and innovators in the modes of global belonging" (pp. 9–10).

If this position is correct, as I believe it to be, then this gives culture (and in this context the arts in particular) a powerful creative function in relation to social transformation, especially in situations where it can capture new visions of the world, and "initiate situations in which artists and public participants are engaged in the mediation of new forms of cosmopolitan agency" (p. 11). This it can do through the deployment of critical imagination, its ability to engage with hybridity and cultural translation, to conceive of alternatives, to reimagine our modes of participation in the world. Art then does not simply follow society, but "Rather, it seeks to create an understanding of new cultural possibilities by allowing each partner to go beyond their own certitudes and participate in collaborative knowledge-making that is not just the sum of their previous experiences" (p. 174). Papastergiadis' argument has many implications—the importance in cultural policy of *training* the imagination, the ways in which artistic experiments can stand against the politics of fear, exclusion and refusal of hospitality, the essential role of aesthetics in forming images of the world, images that in turn form the basis for action, the ability to conceive of new forms of globalism beyond the economic, in particular through acts of cultural translation and cosmopolitanism (Meskimmon 2011): in short, the position of Jacques Ranciere that it is the unique capacity of art to modify "the realm of the visible, the sayable and the possible" (Ranciere 2007: 256–257).

Although Papastergiadis is concerned with the field of contemporary collaborative art, he stands in an extensive tradition of arguments for the socially transformative potential of art. The distinguished Latin American novelist Mario Vargas Llosa for example has written quite extensively on this theme outside of his fiction writing, suggesting, from his own creative experience and from his particular political location that the arts (and his particular field of reference, while including the visual arts is quite naturally literature) enrich life through the imagination in ways that other branches of the humanities including philosophy and sociology cannot. Literature is not simply a by-product of society, but helps constitute it by creating in diverse readers a shared experience, by making them speak to each other, it feeds the critical mind—which is an engine of political change and he best champion of liberty that we have" (Vargas Llosa 2007: 142), provides us with models of the ideal society through allowing an outlet for fantasy and the creative imagination and helps us see where the world is badly made and needs remedying, protests against its misery and injustices and protests against mediocrity. His fellow Latin American Carlos Fuentes, in introducing a collection of Latin American short-stories would concur: "The sheer weight of social problems and quickened change in Latin America have effected and will affect our writing, but will not absolve us from the demand of shaping, giving form, giving speech and imagination, *to* our societies. The political urge manifest in many Latin American writers is explainable: we are citizens and legitimately act as such. But as writers our contribution to society lies less in political action or thematic "correctness" than in the two social needs that a writer is best prepared to fulfill: language and imagination. Deprive a society of its words or its memory, of its speech or its desires, and you are easy prey to *false* illusions, providential leaderships as other traditional ills of Latin American polity (Fuentes 1999: x). Stories then "broaden the field of social behavior to admit new desires, new demands of both the individual and the collective being. They see human beings as both transparent and enigmatic" (ibid., xii)".

The arts then are vehicles of cultural rights, or rather they fulfill this role while *being* the content of culture. The result, sadly not always fulfilled in practice, is a responsibility to broader sociocultural issues, ethics, environment and politics, and the potential ability to form and shape new visions of community and new modes of globalism. Indeed, this international perspective is important: no longer is any culture isolated, new forms of cultural communication through music, film, foods, fashions, tourism (including the rapidly expanding area of "cultural tourism"), and popular culture constantly come into being, and new hybridities, cultural borrowing and appropriation, legitimate or illegitimate, endlessly appear. Culture itself then comes to play a role in international relations. This latter theme in fact has been discussed at length in a book by Roland Bleiker *Aesthetics and World Politics* (Bleiker 2009). Part of Bleiker's argument is by now familiar (although correct one) that good art challenges our habits of representation and so can, ideally, shake us out of perceptual laziness and complacency. The originality of his position is to demonstrate how art can work in this way when applied to the seemingly macro and unpromising field of international relations, a discipline or perspective not noted for its interest in aesthetics, except insofar as "cultural diplomacy" and more recent notions of "soft power" enter into the calculations of politicians. It turns out move over that he not alone in this endeavor, and in fact there is a not inconsiderable literature devoted to the relationship between the arts and international relations, a literature that he surveys and synthesizes, noting that there has been something of an "aesthetic turn" in the field in the last decade and a half (Bleiker 2009: 34–35). This is important for issues of cultural rights and cultural justice as at the very beginning of his book he asks the unavoidable question "Is it trivial, even irresponsible, to explore aesthetic themes at a time when the world is engulfed by war, genocide, terrorism, poverty, climate change and financial turmoil?" (Bleiker 2009: 1), and not surprisingly he answers that it is actually necessary to do so. This does not imply a "political art" of the Socialist Realist type once found in the Soviet Union and China, and to some extent still in North Korea, but rather forms of art that promote imagination, emphasize the links between aesthetics, ethics and politics, challenge dogma, encourage empathy, reject determinism, cultivate a sense of possibility, wonder and enchantment, dilute our obsession with control and challenge the subtle forms of oppression that can be deeply entrenched in language and images. *Cultural activism* then lies at the root of social and political change, and the arts help us realize that our species-being exceeds an identification with the sociopolitical, but also includes our imaginative lives, rest, leisure, access to nature, and, something rarely discussed in the context of rights, development or social transformation, the erotic. Bleiker locates his argument in relation to his own field of international relations, but it could be rephrased in terms of globalization and its cultural aspects, for as John Tomlinson has aptly put it "Globalization lies at the heart of modern culture; cultural practices lie at the heart of globalization" (Tomlinson 2000: 1), and/or in terms of the more anthropological dimensions of cross-cultural encounters and their ontological dimensions when both questions of representation and communication are raised (Clammer et al. 2004), drawing attention back to the specifically cultural dimensions of international relations, which go far beyond the merely political.

The Aesthetics of Justice/the Aesthetics of Development

Justice is often thought of purely in legal terms, but here I am arguing that it has a much wider frame of reference that includes the cultural in all its dimensions—not merely access *to* culture, but equally the responsibility *of* cultural expressions to seek justice both externally, and internally in the sense of integrity and value-creation within any particular cultural field. The older 'human needs' approach would certainly suggest that there is a close connection—basically that human beings have aesthetic needs as well as material ones, and indeed, that the two are connected through ideas of beauty. Much "development" is both violent and produces ugliness—unattractive cities, ruined countryside, substandard housing and design of everyday objects—when this need not be the case, as was demonstrated decades ago by the Bauhaus movement in Germany and the architects and designers that it inspired. The unnecessary destruction of heritage in the name of development is yet another aspect of this. It might indeed be argued that the preservation of heritage, both for the current generation and future ones to enjoy, and as the embodiment of history and memory, whether such heritage be tangible or intangible (Smith and Akagawa 2009). The preservation of such heritage in museums is also crucial, bearing in mind that both heritage and museums are political spaces, and contested ones in terms of what should be displayed, how it should be labeled and what story of the past and its connection to the present is being told (Hooper-Greenhill 1992; Wolf and Wolf 2015). Again an international quasi-legal instrument exists in the form of the 1972 World Heritage Convention, but one frequently honored in the breach rather than in its systematic fulfillment, or ignored altogether as has happened in many circumstances such as in Syria and Afghanistan. Intangible culture heritage is even more fragile by its very nature, being expressed in such media as music, storytelling and performance, particularly of theatre and dance, and while a Convention exists to recognize, support and preserve such forms (UNESCO 2003), few governments which are signatories actually have agencies devoted to that task. Both development thinking and "justice thinking" should be concerned with what *can be*, not only with what currently *is*: with shaping the future as much as describing the empirical outcome of contemporary trends. This is why Allen Kaplan among others has suggested that development is an art, one that requires listening as much as speaking, and requiring intuition, co-creating and imagination more than technical skills (Kaplan 2002). The reasons so many well-meaning development projects fail may be traced precisely to the violation of this principle. Furthermore, such an approach enables an important link to be made between aesthetics, justice and the environment.

The emergent field of eco-criticism is one significant area in which this is materialized. As Timothy Clark suggests in his introduction to the *Cambridge Introduction to Literature and the Environment* (Clark 2011), new tools are needed to conceptualize and engage with the multiple factors driving the accelerating degradation of the environment. Since culture has a "context"—i.e. nature—it is important for the various branches of the cultural studies (including literature) both to relate themselves to the environment and to challenge the conventional categories through which human knowledge is organized, such as the division between the natural sciences, social sciences and the humanities. As he puts it: "In sum, ecocriticism makes up an arena of an exciting and imponderable intersection of issues, intellectual disciplines and politics. Its potential force is not to be just another subject of literary criticism, situated within its given institutional borders, but work engaged provocatively both with literary analysis and with issues that are simultaneously but obscurely matters of science, morality, politics and aesthetics" (Clark 2011: 8). In this context he cites Robert Harrison's notion of "poetic history"—the view that the arts are indeed a privileged site in which assumptions about or definitions of nature and the human and their relationships can be made perceptible in new ways and interrogated accordingly (Clark 2011: 61, citing Harrison 1992), including areas that normally fall outside of our "ecological habitus" as it were, such as the atmosphere, something actually vital to our life and lives, but which is rarely the subject of social science or literary analysis, except perhaps as the weather or the sky in landscape paintings. Clark summarizes his whole argument by stating that "The non-human effects both a de-familiarization of human perception, an undermining of 'speciesism' and a potentially revolutionary ethical appeal against the brutal human tyranny over the animal kingdom" (Clark 2011: 199). Consequently, issues of ethics, aesthetics, environment and cultural practice are simultaneously engaged, and this convergence creates a new model for thinking about development, justice and cultural values, one with considerable transformative potential.

An instance of this that brings together art, literature, architecture and environment (in particular climate change) is Malcolm Miles' investigation into the links between these elements (Miles 2014), and makes many practical suggestions including the revival of crafts, the reclamation of industrially damaged landscapes, eco-villages and interrogates the role of art in these and in other spheres of response to climate change and ecological degradation. Invoking Marcuse, Miles argues that the cultural cannot be separated from the political or economic, and that consequently new cultural norms are necessary to begin the positive reconstruction of our relationship to both the natural and social worlds. In a lesser known article, Marcuse, unlike many others on the Left of his times, argued for an art that fulfilled the fourfold task of advancing beauty, promoting non-violence and serenity and protecting the environment, all of which he saw as necessary tasks in completing what might be called a "holistic" revolution—one concerned with matters well beyond only the economic and political as they are conventionally understood (Marcuse 1972/2005).

Necessary too is an understanding of history, and it is significant that the expanding field of post-colonial studies/post-colonial criticism has begun to address not only issues of the relationship between colonialism and the arts, as pioneered by the work of Edward Said (1993), but also the triangular relationship between colonialism, the arts (in particular literature) and the environment (for example Cilano and DeLoughrey 2007; Huggan and Tiffin 2010). Colonialism of course not only had profound effects on local languages and literatures—and on the visual arts and modes of performance (Mitter 2007)—but also on local ecologies, transforming forest and swamp into plantations, introducing new plant and animal species, promoting new forms of urbanization, and encouraging new diets that in turn profoundly influenced what might be eaten and hence cultivated or reared. "Ecological imperialism" (Cosby 1986) does not just transform many aspects of the physical environment in colonized (and in colonizing countries), but also the ways in which those transformed environments are perceived and so represented, mourned, celebrated or memorialized and reflected in art and performance. Implicit in this is a concern with rights—of the biosphere as a whole or of particular categories within it, such as animals. Given that the cultures and languages of indigenous peoples embody large quantities of ecological knowledge, cultural preservation and the preservation of the environment go hand-in-hand. This of course raises another complex question—that of the historical violation of rights and of restitution for those violations, an issue that is now powerfully reemerging in the context of the responsibility for climate change, and one calling into question what might indeed be an essential yet limited conception of rights embodied in the foundational Universal Declaration of Human Rights which with hindsight might not have been sufficiently sensitive to cultural differences, and as yet unaware of the growing significance of animal rights and the perilous state of the global environment. Since the environment is the ultimate context of all human activity, cultural rights need to be situated within this setting, not least to avoid the possible excesses of a purely anthropocentric worldview and the art that arises from such a limited perspective.

Cultural Action for Justice

In his introduction to the 1999 edition of the annual United Nations Development Program report, Mahbub ul Haq points out that "The purpose of development is to create an enabling environment for people to enjoy long, healthy, creative lives. This simple but powerful truth is often forgotten in the pursuit of material and financial wealth" (UNDP 1999: 1). In such a conception of development culture is clearly central, but not just any culture, but expressions that enhance life, create and reinforce positive values, stand against violence, suggest now perceptions and modes of being and representation, which deeply respect nature and which build convivial communities, even when those communities are transitory. All societies are made up of and operate through networks of symbolic systems—language, representations embodied in art, crafts, objects, architecture and fashion, mythology and the expression of history, often in material form in museums, religions, music and various forms of science, including local ethnosciences. Embodied in all these "systems" are aesthetic norms and practices, including concepts of beauty, proportion and "rightness". In a sense then, holistic development means not only the creation of material wealth and well-being (expressed in such institutional forms as education and health care), but the enrichment of culture—the deepening of our symbolic systems to bring them into congruence with our real needs and potentials, and with the imperatives of nature, which set the context and limits of any human practices.

It follows from this that cultural activism is necessary for the pursuit of cultural justice. This is not in itself a new idea—Paolo Freire long ago, based on his revolutionary approach to literacy acquisition, argued for cultural action for freedom (Freire 1972). It needs to be understood, as the art scholar Shannon Jackson has rightly pointed out, that a great deal of cultural criticism sees itself as deconstructive, while what is equally needed is *constructive* theory and activism which leads to the reconstruction of culture and its energizing as a path of social transformation (Jackson 2011). The concept of "environmental racism" is now well established. This approach now needs to be extended to the idea of "aesthetic racism", or for that matter to "classism"—the exclusion of people of any ethnicity, social status defined in terms of class or caste, gender or age—from access to natural and cultural beauty. This is the core idea of the notion of "visual justice"—essentially the right to beauty. This in turn can be extended to aural, olfactory, and other forms of sensory justice such as the right not to be exposed to noise pollution, light pollution or other forms of sensory violence. This merges slowly but seamlessly into environmental justice—the right to clean and unpolluted spaces and landscapes—and to food justice—the right of access to adequate and healthy nutrition. Cultural justice is consequently a very inclusive term, and one which strongly suggests that the notion of human rights be extended far beyond its narrow legalistic definition. This has two outcomes—to *protect* a wider range of rights, and by defining unexpected areas of culture as arena of rights, to *encourage* the recognition of those areas as ones requiring creative work in pursuit of social transformation. Development is often violent, both in its direct effects on people sociologically and economically (displacement, de-skilling, marginalization), but also culturally in the erosion of indigenous cultures and their replacement by hegemonic global ones reflecting values at radical variance with the ones desirable for sustainability and humanization. Cultural action for justice is then equally the struggle for a holistic development: the two are inseparable. The detailed discussion of the nature of such cultural action will be taken up in the concluding chapter.

This suggests the desirability of not only polycentric aesthetics reflecting the empirical diversity of cultures and ever evolving forms of hybridity, but also the *celebration* of difference, and the need for a *transformative aesthetics* not simply a descriptive one. Development is not a simply technical process or one reducible to economics, but an art, and the principal arena of a struggle over values. A poetics of development is essential, and it is only through the medium of a genuinely humanized and "naturized" (ecological) culture that such a mind and imagination expanding goal can be achieved. It is at this point that a dialogue between the arts and development emerges at many possible levels—in the context of debates about "culture and development", in the goals of organizations like UNESCO to promote "creative industries" as pathways to economic development, in shifting attention to not so much culture *and* development, but the *development of culture* as one of the principal goals of holistic development, and in appreciating the myriad ways—through film theatre, dance, the visual arts, poetry and the novel—the whole experience of development is refracted and it's all too frequent violence addressed as lives become pawns in colonial, political and globalized forces that they suffer even as others may benefit from those same processes (Clammer 2015). As Suvir Kaul has shown in his beautiful and sensitive book on Kashmir, a highly contested area of divided between India and Pakistan and harbouring at least three major religions (Islam, Hinduism and Buddhism), that poetry in particular, among the possible "artistic" expressions of culture, has been a powerful means of "cultural work" addressing the endemic violence, militarization, distorted "development", political myopia and above all the tragic loss of life, much of it entirely innocent, that has characterized the region since Partition (of India and Pakistan) in 1947. As he puts it in summarizing many of the specific conclusions of his book "In times of such disorientation, literary writing is a powerful indicator of the way social transitions are lived by individuals and communities. Its affective range encompasses both the raw immediacy of testimonials of victims and witnesses of brutal events, and the more mediated, longer-term, reflections that they precipitate. In particular, the formal structures of literary writing often enable the staging of intense human experiences that are outside the rhetorical norms of other forms of reportage" (Kaul 2017: 135). Now that issues of sustainability are at the forefront of public and academic discourse, the place of the arts in encouraging a world of ecological sensitivity, social justice, spaces of freedom and broad-based creativity, and of the arts themselves becoming part of that process and reflecting those values and goals, is ever more required (Clammer and Giri 2017). Cultural justice must mean both justice within cultures and justice between cultures as the medium in which humans live, and the wider biosphere, which not only informs the patterns which culture can take, but in the final analysis forms the unavoidable conditions which any culture must accept if it is to survive.

References

Armstrong, John. 2005. *The Secret Power of Beauty*. London: Penguin Books.

Becker, Carol. 1994. Herbert Marcuse and the Subversive Potential of Art. In *The Subversive Imagination: Artists, Society, and Social Responsibility*, ed. Carol Becker, 113–129. New York and London: Routledge.

Berger, John. 1977. *Ways of Seeing*. London: Penguin Books.

Bermudez, Jose Luis, and Sebastian Gardner (eds.). 2003. *Art and Morality*. London and New York: Routledge.

Bleiker, Roland. 2009. *Aesthetics and World Politics*. Basingstoke and New York: Palgrave Macmillan.

Brady, Emile. 2003. *Aesthetics of the Natural Environment*. Edinburgh: Edinburgh University Press.

Budd, Malcolm. 2005. *The Aesthetic Appreciation of Nature: Essays on the Aesthetics of Nature*. Oxford: Clarendon Press.

Cilano, Cara, and Elizabeth DeLonghrey. 2007. Against Authenticity: Global Knowledge and Postcolonial Ecocriticism. *Interdisciplinary Studies in Literature and the Environment* 14 (1): 71–86.

Clammer, John. 2009. Beyond Power: Alternative Conceptions of Being and the Reconstitution of Social Theory. In *The Modern Prince and the Modern Sage: Transforming Power and Freedom*, ed. A.K. Giri, 559–575. New Delhi and Los Angeles: Sage.

Clammer, John. 2014. *Vision and Society: Towards a Sociology and Anthropology from Art*. London and New York: Routledge.

Clammer, John. 2015. *Art, Culture and International Development: Humanizing Social Transformation*. London and New York: Routledge.

Clammer, John, and Ananta Kumar Giri (eds.). 2017. *The Aesthetics of Development: Art, Culture and Social Transformation*. Basingstoke and New York: Palgrave Macmillan.

Clammer, John, Sylvie Poirier, and Eric Schwimmer (eds.). 2004. *Figured Worlds: Ontological Obstacles in Intercultural Relations*. Toronto and London: University of Toronto Press.

Clark, Timothy. 2011. *The Cambridge Introduction to Literature and the Environment*. Cambridge: Cambridge University Press.
Cosby, Alfred W. 1986. *Ecological Imperialism: The Biological Expansion of Europe, 900–1900*. Cambridge: Cambridge University Press.
Cushing, Lincoln. 2003. *!Revolution!: Cuban Poster Art*. San Francisco: Chronicle Books.
Dutton, Denis. 2010. *The Art Instinct: Beauty, Pleasure, and Human Evolution*. London: Bloomsbury.
Elias, Norbert. 1978. *The Civilizing Process: The History of Manners*, vol. 1. Oxford: Basil Blackwell.
Fischer, Ernst. 2010. *The Necessity of Art*, trans. Anna Bostock, with an Introduction by John Berger. London and New York: Verso.
Freire, Paolo. 1972. *Cultural Action for Freedom*. Harmondsworth: Penguin Books.
Fuentes, Carlos. 1999. The Storyteller. In *The Picador Book of Latin American Stories*, ed. Carlos Fuentes and Julio Ortega. London: Picador.
Ghosh, Amitav. 2016. *The Great Derangement: Climate Change and the Unthinkable*. Gurgaon: Allen Lane India.
Gomez-Pena, Guillermo. 1994. The Free Art Agreement/El Tratado de Libre Cultura. In *The Subversive Imagination: Artists, Society and Social Responsibility*, ed. Carol Becker, 208–222. New York and London: Routledge.
Harrison, Roger P. 1992. *Forests: The Shadow of Civilization*. Chicago and London: University of Chicago Press.
Holloway, John. 2002. *Change the World Without Taking Power*. London and Ann Arbor: Pluto Press.
Hooper-Greenhill, Eilean (ed.). 1992. *Museums and the Shaping of Knowledge*. London and New York: Routledge.
Huggan, Graham, and Helen Tiffin. 2010. *Postcolonial Ecocriticism: Literature, Animals, Environment*. London and New York: Routledge.
Jackson, Shannon. 2011. *Social Works: Performing Art, Supporting Publics*. New York and London: Routledge.
Kaplan, Allen. 2002. *Development Practitioners and Social Process: Artists of the Invisible*. London: Pluto Press.
Kaul, Suvir. 2017. *Of Gardens and Graves: Kashmir, Poetry, Politics*. Durham, NC and London: Duke University Press.
Kester, Grant H. 2011. *The One and the Many: Contemporary Collaborative Arts in a Global Context*. Durham, NC and London: Duke University Press.
Lederach, John Paul. 2005. *The Moral Imagination: The Art and Soul of Making Peace*. New York and Oxford: Oxford University Press.
Marcuse, Herbert. 1972/2005. Ecology and Revolution. In *The New Left and the 1960s*, ed. D. Kellner, 173–176. London and New York: Routledge.
Marcuse, Herbert. 1978. *The Aesthetic Dimension*. Boston: Beacon Press.

Meskimmon, Marsha. 2011. *Contemporary Art and the Cosmopolitan Imagination*. London and New York: Routledge.

Miles, Malcolm. 2014. *Eco-Aesthetics: Art, Literature and Architecture in a Period of Climate Change*. London and New York: Bloomsbury.

Mitter, Partha. 2007. *The Triumph of Modernism: Indian Artists and the Avant-Garde 1922–1947*. New Delhi: Oxford University Press.

Negri, Antonio. 2012. *Art and Multitude: Nine Letters on Art, Followed by Metamorphoses: Art and Immaterial Labour*, trans. Ed Emery. Cambridge and Malden, MA: Polity Press.

Nussbaum, Martha C. 1995. *Poetic Justice: The Literary Imagination and Public Life*. Boston: Beacon Press.

Nussbaum, Martha C. 2012. *Not for Profit: Why Democracy Needs the Humanities*. Princeton and London: Princeton University Press.

Oz, Amos. 1983. *In the Land of Israel*. London: Flamingo.

Palmer, Frank. 1992. *Literature and Moral Understanding: A Philosophical Essay on Ethics, Aesthetics, Education and Culture*. Oxford: Clarendon Press.

Papastergiadis, Nikos. 2012. *Cosmopolitanism and Culture*. Cambridge and Malden, MA: Polity Press.

Ranciere, Jacques. 2004. *The Politics of Aesthetics*, ed. and trans. Gabriel Rockhill. London and New York: Bloomsbury.

Ranciere, Jacques. 2007. Art of the Possible: Fulvia Carnevale and John Kelsey in Conversation with Jacques Ranciere. *Art Forum International* 45 (7): 256–266.

Roszak, Theodore, Mary E. Gomes, and Allen D. Kanner (eds.). 1995. *Ecopsychology: Restoring the Earth, Healing the Mind*. San Francisco: Sierra Club Books.

Rothenberg, David. 2011. *Survival of the Beautiful: Art, Science and Evolution*. London and New York: Bloomsbury.

Said, Edward W. 1993. *Culture and Imperialism*. London: Chatto and Windus.

Scarry, Elaine. 2000. *On Beauty and Being Just*. London: Gerald Duckworth.

Smith, L., and N. Akagawa (eds.). 2009. *Intangible Heritage*. London and New York: Routledge.

Tomlinson, John. 2000. *Globalization and Culture*. Cambridge: Polity Press.

UNDP (United Nations Development Program). 1999. *Human Development Report 1999*. New York: UNDP and Oxford University Press.

UNESCO (United Nations Educational, Scientific and Cultural Organization). 2003. *Convention on the Safeguarding of the Intangible Cultural Heritage*. Paris: UNESCO.

Vargas Llosa, Mario. 2007. *Touchstones: Essays on Literature, Art and Politics*. London: Faber and Faber.

Wolf, Arun, and Gita Wolf (eds.). 2015. *Between Memory and Museum: A Dialogue with Folk and Tribal Arts*. Chennai and London: Tara Books.

CHAPTER 7

The Right to Peace? Cultural Values, Peace and Conflict Resolution

Is the right to peace a cultural right along with other more immediately recognizable ones? It can certainly be argued that no true, lasting or holistic development can take place in the absence of peace. In discussing peace in its relationship with broader development issues, existential questions also arise—why is every conception of utopia one of lasting peace, while the common reality of our societies is of violence and conflict? So, discussing peace and conflict issues, and indeed issues of violence in general, makes little sense without considering the sociological and cultural factors involved. This chapter will attempt to provide a broad sociological model of peace and conflict and social violence in general, and attempt to relate them both to authentic development and to the question of cultural rights, and will essentially argue that no notion of holistic of just conception of such development is possible (in terms of economic and social justice, gender and relationships to nature) without consideration to questions of peace, and without further integrating peace studies into development studies, the two fields having inexplicably drifted apart. Certainly, the argument has been made that peace is a human right, and one necessary for the flourishing of any sustained forms of cultural expression (UNESCO 1997a).

This approach has several elements—identifying the sources of conflict, exploring case studies of actual recent conflict situations, debating the extent to which these are linked to issues of social maldevelopment, and from these building a model of a sociology of conflict and its relationship to traditional mechanisms of peace maintenance and conflict

J. Clammer, *Cultural Rights and Justice*,
https://doi.org/10.1007/978-981-13-2811-4_7

resolution. These factors suggest a potentially rich role for legal and political anthropology. The chapter will briefly explore the relationship between peace and human security and the holistic nature of the establishment of peace and of the factors which structure such an environment. Stress will in particular be given to the linkages between different sociocultural (including ethnic and religious), economic and political levels and the question of how these are articulated. The paper will reintroduce the older notion of social disorganization, the issues that empirical and sociological studies of peace and conflict suggest, and the methodological ways in which anthropology can be employed both as an analytical technique and as a source of case studies and ethnographic record. Such a model may have some predictive power in anticipating possible future sources of conflict. Galtung has proposed a model of a triangular relationship between "structural", "cultural" and "direct" forms of violence, and this chapter will propose ways in which that model can be applied and also refined and developed, and of how it relates to both culture and development and to the relationship between them.

Cultural Approaches to Peace and Conflict

The distinguished peace studies scholar Johan Galtung has proposed a tripartite model for analyzing and understanding situations of peace and conflict, one involving a triangular relationship between what he calls structural, direct and cultural violence. Structural violence refers to such situations as practices and effects emerging from systematic forms of social inequality such as caste, or at a global level, the exclusions or actual generation of poverty resulting from many forms of globalization (trade practices for example). Direct violence is that embodied in war or in the forms of violence that accompany many revolutions. Cultural violence is that to be found coded into many of our human cultural practices—unequal gender relationships, tolerated economic inequalities, extreme rituals of initiation and punishment including executions, bodily mutilations, cannibalism, crime, and the multiple forms of racism, sexism, ageism and other modes of social exclusion which human societies have developed over history. Also to be included here might be human relationships to nature when they are exploitative, extractive and damaging to both other species which inhabit the planet with us, and to the biosphere as a whole through the imposition of pollution for example on many innocent victims who have nothing to do with the production of the toxins in the first place. Today a paramount example of this would be climate change, massive physical changes in the Earth's atmosphere generated by the few, but imposed without their consent on the many (Galtung 1975, 1990).

In this chapter I will focus on the cultural dimensions of this model and, while not taking issue with Galtung's basic model, will suggest that it needs expanding and deepening to include a number of cross-cutting factors, anthropological, sociological and psychological, that make its application to actual situations more effective. The approach to violence and conflict through culture is vital. Culture is the "medium" in which as humans we live our lives. It structures and is the source of our ideas about space: personal space, boundaries national and social, sacred and secular spaces, nature, memory-spaces, architecture and many other dimensions of our physical being in the world (Lefebvre 1991), of time (seasons, significant dates of festivals, commemorations, life cycle events), dress, foods, our relationships to the transcendental (religion and forms of spirituality), our relationships with objects (through art and though consumerism) and our understandings of relationships (kinship, friendship, enemies, rivals). It is the source of most that is good in our lives, but also of most of what is violent and destructive outside of the forces of pure nature—crime, punishment, wars, forms of entertainment such as violent movies and video games and even sports, to say nothing of patterns of destructive personal behavior—domestic and sexual violence, "honor killings" and the many forms of dishonesty that humans have so creatively discovered.

In expanding his own tripartite model, Galtung has suggested that there are four "spaces" that produce either peace or violence—the space of personal relationships, the social one of culture, politics and economy, the global space of world systems and the ecological space in which people interact with nature. In practice, these four "spaces" are closely interconnected and interact with one another to produce zones of peace and conflict. One significant way of creating a model of peace and conflict is to develop these suggestions in two directions—one a holistic one of creating an interactive "systems" model in which all the elements are kept in balance, and the other is to fill out these categories and to supplement them with additional insights. I will, while keeping in mind the need for holism, concentrate more on the latter, focusing throughout on the role of culture, and attempting to demonstrate how an expanded cultural approach, in particular drawing on anthropology, can provide an enriched picture of peace and conflict situations. In doing so, I will also suggest ways in which anthropology itself can be deepened in an attempt to grasp what I will here call the "deep cultural grammar" of conflict and post-conflict situations and hence recover its role in speaking to "development" situations.

A Social Model of Peace and Conflict

I have argued at length elsewhere (Clammer 2015) that peace and social development are closely connected, as are successful post-conflict reconciliation and lasting peace situations. Social development means of course a range of things, but the essential ones in this context can be defined as equity in the distribution of resources, combatting the erosion of autonomy or perceived threats to these especially when this is the situation of ethnic or religious minorities, diminishment of poverty and large income differentials, combatting the negative effects of globalization such as price volatility for locally produced commodities (e.g. coffee, rubber latex, cocoa and other primary products), threats to cultural integrity, and promoting access to education, health care and other common goods to the widest range of a population regardless of ethnicity, gender, caste or other sociocultural divisions. The analysis of recent conflict situations around the globe shows that these are key factors, but so are others that often are regarded as outside of conventional social analysis.

These include perceived religious differences (Protestant-Catholic conflict in Northern Ireland, Christian-Muslim rivalry as in the former Yugoslavia), old tribal differences often based on territorial ambitions (as currently in South Sudan), clashes of political ideologies, the long-term effects of colonial history and, very frequently, land-grabbing or the desire for territory currently occupied by others (as in Israel, Rwanda, or in conflicts between mainly Javanese transmigrants and indigenous Papuans in the Indonesian province of Irian Jaya). In other words, while conflict is often ascribed to ethnic and/or religious differences, almost inevitably these are underpinned by other factors of a more material or political nature. "Development" is a process that can generate its own new inequalities, and so fair development must be understood in terms of development that is equitable and which shares its fruits equally across communities and the individual members of those communities. So either unequal development or the absence of fair development can create the conditions for conflict, and will undermine any lasting post-conflict settlement. This points to a model with four levels. The first is that of global and usually (in Galtung's terms) structural factors—international currency fluctuations, capital flight, Structural Adjustment or austerity programs imposed by lenders of the multilateral financial institutions (as was vividly demonstrated in Greece in the recent past), all of which can have wildly destabilizing effects on local societies. The second is sociological and relates to such factors as unequal access to land, historical patterns of ethnic exclusion, often with their roots in slavery, forced migrations, the lingering effects of colonialism on language, access to economic, political or educational resources and to internal factors within a given community such as gender relations, caste, class, patriarchy, the material bases of religious differences, differential landholdings or property inequalities, tribal distinctions and unequal abilities to exercise social power as a result of differences in cultural as well as economic capital. The third is anthropological and points to the mechanisms through which societies have long utilized to settle disputes, mediate conflicts, deal with issues such as succession and inheritance, punish those deemed to be criminals, and to ensure that warfare, if it should break out, is of low intensity and short duration and may even be largely symbolic, with few casualties on either side (Roberts 1979). Also linked to this area of legal and political anthropology are issues of the relationship between human rights and the kinds of societies that anthropologists have largely chosen to study, and in which notions of rights may be rooted in very different sociological and cultural contexts than that envisaged by the authors of the Universal Declaration of Human Rights (Wilson 1997; Cowan et al. 2001). But the fourth, which I will now go on to elaborate, takes us to a further level, one which in many cases provides the deep grammar for more surface manifestations of conflict that often appear as ethnic or religious.

Memory Work

While access to the fruits of development, or denial of them while others are obviously benefiting, is then certainly a factor in peace and conflict and levels of social violence, it is certainly not the only factor at work. For there are clearly societies with "low" levels of development as defined by such indicators as the human development index which do not manifest conflict, while others, with demonstrably higher levels, do. So the "level" of development is not a predictor of conflict, although it is clearly a contributing factor. Other factors must be at work, and here I will suggest that they are to be found in what I will call "memory work": the development, manipulation and social use of memories, false or constructed, which are then used for largely political ends. Examples of this abound, and are not necessarily negative (contemporary memorialization of the Holocaust for example). I recall on a visit to Northern Ireland seeing sprayed on a wall the words "Remember 1688", something that clearly no one alive today in Ireland or anywhere else is able to do. This of course refers to a "historical memory"—the keeping alive through public memorialization of an event in the distant past (the imposition of the Protestant Prince William of Orange on the Catholic Irish by the hated English overlords). Such memorialization can be found embodied in quite literal concrete memorials (cenotaphs, statues of the heroes of some war or revolution), in school textbooks (a source of endless dispute between Korea and China and Japan), in popular literature, in history books of varying degrees of accuracy and ideological bias, in films and in the rhetoric of nationalism (which almost always has to pitch the in-group against sometimes demonized others), in the mass media, and in the sermons delivered from the pulpits of churches, mosques, synagogues and temples. Paradoxically, regions with a long history of actual friendly coexistence on the ground, often harbor the most virulent propaganda at the political or state level, as again in parts of the former Yugoslavia, although such situations can be highly unstable, as in Poland during the Second World War, where, despite the depredations of Nazi occupation, there are many recorded examples of Catholic Poles turning on and turning in, their Jewish neighbors, with whom they had lived peacefully for generations, a situation tragically paralleled in Rwanda half a century later where Tutsi and Hutu slaughtered those who they knew well and had lived alongside peacefully for many years, or in Indonesia in the intervening period when under the guise of an anti-communist rising, many old scores were bloodily settled, a legacy that even now the country is only just beginning to come to terms with.

The recognition that memory is socially constructed, and that those constructions have political and ideological uses has since the 1990s become an important area of sociological and anthropological research (e.g. Connerton 1995; Freeman 1993). Here again there are a number of levels, ranging from the literal social construction of memory (and with it identity) as in Benedict Anderson's now classic study of the manufacturing of nationalism, largely through the print media (Anderson 1993), right through all intermediate levels until we reach the hidden injuries and resentments that arise so easily from not only the more obvious forms of social inequality and injustice, but also from the everyday life experiences and structures that so many people are forced to experience—exclusions, being ignored, lack of recognition, rejections obvious or more subtle (O'Brian and Howard 1998). In their more extreme forms, these become the sources of trauma and as such both the potential causes of violence and often its effect. I have elsewhere examined in much more detail the sociology of trauma, and its relationship to remembering and its close cousin, forgetting, in the context of negotiating the experience of social violence, and how these in turn are linked to narratives—of the ways in which both victims and perpetrators of social violence relate and justify their stories, and of how these might in turn be related to mechanisms of healing and reconciliation (Clammer 2012: 192–219). Here I will draw on that research in the context of peace and conflict studies in order to illustrate the connections between such studies and memory work.

Conflict often arises from resentment, a phrase that was once common in French social theory, but which appears to have dropped out of regular usage. This can lead to individual outbursts of anger and violence, but my primary concern here is with societies rather than individuals and the ways in which they collectively both memorialize and edit, suppress or attempt to enhance, either memories of their own violence, or of their suffering. Remembering, forgetting and mythologizing thus constitute another triangulation of processes, and both can be practiced by victims and victimizers alike. It is important to remember in this context that conflict may not take overtly violent forms—aspects of development itself, especially perception of rising inequalities, displacement, loss of ancestral lands or forests, subjection to inappropriate education—can constitute examples of "chronic" violence as opposed to the "acute" varieties that typically arise in war or other overtly violent situations, or the forms of suffering that may arise from natural disasters. Formal memorialization, while itself inevitably represents a particular reading of history (a statue of Queen Victoria in India will be read rather differently from a similar statue in London; the column on which is perched a statue of Admiral Lord Nelson in the center of Trafalgar Square will have a rather different significance to a French person than to an English one). And such formal memorials are usually the prerogative of the state, it being largely only in the cemetery that private citizens are allowed to raise memorials, and then only to their personal dead, and such memorials are likely to be of only modest size and of a specifically religious character.

But while heroes (itself a relative term) and public figures may be embodied in stone or bronze, the suffering of those without voices is likely to go unmarked, or, and more dangerously for long-term peace, co-opted for a national or political project. In her study of the literatures of trauma, Kali Tal raises the important question of what happens when such stories are co-opted and retold, not by the victims themselves, but by others purporting to speak on their behalf, when they are "adapted to fit and then contained within the dominant structure of cultural and political discourse?" (Tal 1996: 3), and her answer is that they become "written and rewritten until they become codified and narrative form gradually replaces content as the focus of attention" (Tal 1996: 6). This is not only true of the narratives of actual survivors or, less commonly, perpetrators, of violence, but is a besetting problem of history writing. History, usually offering itself as an objective account of past events and explanation of causality, is actually the most ideologically laden branch of the humanities, in which interpretation is inevitable, and that process of interpretation subject to not only personal biases, but very much to current political and ideological ones, fashionable modes of representation, the expectations of publishers and the reading public and even the scissors of censors. As Edward Said so classically demonstrated a generation ago, visual and literary representations are very much part of how the "Other" is depicted, and so conceived of and related to, often in negative ways (Said 1985), and subsequent studies have shown how significant the visual field and visual culture are in the ways in which the world is perceived, edited and acted upon (Mirzoeff 2015).

Such "alternative" memories can then become the source of social conflict, but much depends on the relative power of victims and victimizers, and of the ways in which they have preserved, manufactured or utilized those memories. The international Jewish community is quite powerful enough to keep the story (true memories are fading as actual aged survivors die off) of the Holocaust very much alive, an event now the subject of endless books, testimonies, films, sites of memory and even comics. But this memorialization has not become a source of conflict with Germany, precisely because the Germans also keep the story alive in a different way and as painfully acknowledged aspect of their history. The former concentration camps are now sites of a kind of secular pilgrimage undertaken voluntarily by many Germans and required of high school students. The same however cannot be said of the Turkish holocaust of Armenians, an event vehemently denied in the country in which it was perpetrated, but very much kept alive in the Armenian diaspora, where what seems to be sought is mainly an admission of guilt, not material reparations of some kind. But paradoxically the Holocaust as the central historical trauma of recent Jewish history, is often turned against Zionist settlers in Israel by Palestinian Arabs, who see the Jews as now perpetrating a slower version against themselves, not through death camps, but through displacement of people from their ancestral lands, border controls, the relegation of Israeli Arabs to second-class citizenship, illegal settlement on Palestinian land and military control. Such historical injustices run deep and it behooves contemporary politicians to think carefully before committing or allowing such acts, for seed sown today may bear an evil fruit far into the future, with generations or even centuries of conflict springing from an unwise decision today.

The model being proposed here then has several elements that we might now summarize. These are (1) The intersection between "objective" events (earlier conflicts, displacements, mal-development, exclusions, injustices) and "memories" of those events, whether actual, invented, mythologized or politically manipulated. (2) That those who control public memorialization cannot move in the direction of conflict without mobilizing the real or perceived resentments of those who believe that they have been victimized or suffered and have not received any just compensation. In this way the study of conflict intersects with the sociology and anthropology of social movements in numerous ways, including the question of how people are mobilized to act on grievances, of how to sustain such mobilization, of how to institutionalize the outcomes of successful mobilizations, and of how to define a grievance in the first place in a sufficiently strong way to cause people not only to act, but potentially to undertake acts that might require substantial sacrifices on their part. (3) The psychological sources of sense of injustice, a state of excitation, a belief in heroic action and/or of sacrifice as the way to achieve the desired goal which may be the restoration of a previous state of which one has been deprived, or the desire for a victory over a perceived enemy. The theory that sport is a kind of sublimated or socially approved form of conflict may not be so far off the mark here. (4) The status of victim is an ambiguous one. On the one hand, it may give a certain kind of moral power (I/we have been wronged and deserve justice or recompense), but on the other, it may represent a status of weakness, of liminality (especially when the line between victim and victimizer is blurred as with Vietnam War veterans in the United States, or with victims of the A-Bombings of Hiroshima and Nagasaki, it often being forgotten that Hiroshima was a major military base and the home headquarters of the Japanese 6th Army, which was busy carrying out atrocities in China). A victim may thus be doubly victimized—a survivor of the original atrocity or event which first created that status, and someone not necessarily welcomed back into the society from which she or he has come, when that status is a reminder of events that the rest of society would rather suppress. As Eric Leed aptly puts it in his book on the identity problems of survivors of First World War trench warfare "He derives all his features from the fact that he has crossed the boundaries of distinctive social worlds, from peace to war, and back. He has been re-shaped by his voyage along the margins of civilization, a voyage in which he has been presented with wonders, curiosities and monsters – things that can only be guessed at by those who remain at home" (Leed 1979: 193–194). The liminality of the survivor then becomes the source of further resentment, and so the cycle continues.

There are parallels here with the outcomes of studies of the survivors of natural disasters—although also important differences. The major difference of course is that it is difficult in most cases to ascribe such a disaster to a specific human agent, even though many "natural" disasters are actually the result of prior human actions—deforestation on wooded hillsides leading to landslides and flooding in the regions below, bad dam construction or the presence of the dam itself. But the sense of, and actual objective conditions of, loss may well be the same as in situations of destruction through violence, and the narrative strategies of survivors of both natural and social violence have many common structural features. This means that the "objective" (sociological, economic, ecological, ethnic, religious, political) factors that may engender conflict need to be balanced with an interpretative one that, as I have suggested elsewhere "retains the centrality of subjectivities, intersubjectivity and reflexivity, in which cognition and emotion, body, selfhood and issues of identity formation and maintenance are all encapsulated" (Clammer 2012: 200). These factors in turn must be located in a situation in which, as Fred Dallmayr argues, despite all the sociological talk of civil society and its wonders, in fact we live in a world of a weakened and diminishing public sphere which can in practice do little to influence or modify political, business or military decisions, often taken in secret and without public knowledge or consent (Dallmayr 2004). A generation earlier, Hannah Arendt had not only argued that public life was becoming progressively colonized by violent practices and ideologies, but also that these were being supported by ideas that were emerging in sociobiology and biological anthropology that suggested that as a species we are congenitally prone to violence and aggression, that this is an integral aspect of human nature, and in some strands of social theory that were suggesting that preoccupation with power is likewise normal and that warfare as a result pertains to the essence of the state (Arendt 1970).

Such a model needs to be tested against actual situations of conflict, including the analysis as suggested above of the progenitors or preconditions of a specific conflict, the factors that sparked the conflict from these factors (since not every situation in which they are present results in a conflict: Quebec and Anglophone Canada have not yet gone to war despite linguistic and religious differences, a conflicting precolonial history and the fact that Quebec is one of the poorest provinces of the country). For it is evident that conflict takes many forms—of war between states, between ethnic or religious groups within a state, between or involving non-state actors such as ISIS, or violence between people in the same community, but led by crime or drug cartels, as in the *favelas* of Brazilian cities or in contemporary Mexico. In some cases, as in the former Yugoslavia, intercommunity conflict was held in abeyance by the strong arm of the Communist state, but with the death of Tito old religious and ethnic rivalries once again reared their heads. Animosities dating back to the Ottoman times were fueled by atrocities perpetrated during the Second World War, and humiliations forced onto people and families that had been on the "wrong" side during the war by the new regime as perpetual "reminders" of that past, leaving no space for reconciliation or closure, leaving a permanent historical running wound in which even monuments to the "other" side were destroyed to, as one informant put it, "Kill the dead" (Bax 2004). This all suggests that one of the key issues is identity, and the desire for recognition of that identity is crucial: underlying many situations of conflict is a politics of recognition. Studies of the vicious conflict between the Tamil and Sinhalese communities in Sri Lanka have shown clearly that violence, certainly on the part of the Tamils, was not a willed outcome, but was the response to not only attacks on literal bodies, but even more so on Tamil notions of dignity and self-respect. The originating trauma (the anti-Tamil riots of 1983) when met by reciprocal violence, began a cycle which, even when met by some victims with silence rather than retaliation (Daniel 1997) leaves its traces for unknown periods of time, unerased by the experience of exile or migration, or even reinforced by them, distance in some cases magnifying rather than diminishing them (Young 1997).

This suggests that conflict is underpinned by a complex psychology, well illustrated by the Sri Lankan case, in which a number of key elements are present. While discriminatory policies on the part of the Sri Lankan government and very unequal development certainly provided the "objective" conditions of conflict, once initiated the conflict began to be read, at least on the part of the Tamils, in much more ontological terms. That is to say as a conflict deeply tied in with notions of pain and exclusion on the one hand, and with the desire for dignity, autonomy and self-respect on the other. To do this in what appeared to be an intolerable situation in which negotiation and normal channels of conflict resolution had been foreclosed, a transformation in the normal expectations of the nature of everyday life had to be achieved. Death had to be seen as a means of recovery not termination in which violent death was not tragedy or to be publically feared, but interpreted as martyrdom and the route to posthumous heroic status. Similarly, violence, normally alien in what had been a conservative and indeed religious community, had to be embraced and projected outwards at the Other, and where necessary inwards to members of one's own community who showed signs of treachery or wavering in the struggle. The construction of the self through violence, while it may be ultimately self-destructive, does quite commonly provide the basis for creating senses of identity, autonomy, masculinity and even freedom. When a social, political or economic situation seems intolerable, provoking or responding with violence may seem to be the only route not only for redressing those absences or deprivations, but for reestablishing a sense of selfhood compatible with deeply held cultural notions of dignity, notions which may in fact prove to be fairly universal.

Here then psychology, history, development, social structure, anthropology and social ontology all come together, into which spaces themselves may be drawn. Locations of atrocities, traumatic events, battlefields, frequently become highly charged memory-sites—places such as Hiroshima or Auschwitz, which attract what Lisa Yoneyama in her study of Hiroshima calls an "excess of memory" (Yoneyama 1999) in which historical interpretations are struggled with and over and in which narratives are reframed and retold—become the concrete sites of memorialization. For even memories need a material rooting, without which they fade and lose any political significance or possibility of exploitation for political ends. "Memoryscapes" and landscapes often need each other: memories need to be embodied to be socially useful. The "taming" of the memoryscape or the emptying them of their historical significance then becomes an important means of removing long-term sources of conflict. It is no accident that newly independent countries frequently begin their new political life by changing street names, removing statues, erecting new monuments to the revolutionary heroes and often redesigning the capital city to spatially reflect its new identity and to symbolically assert its postcolonial status (Kusno 2000).

Beyond Fear

Based on his work in a number of African societies that have experienced civil war and the atrocities—killing, rape, mutilation, burning of villages and destruction of peoples' livelihoods, often without consideration of age or gender, the anthropologist Michael Jackson argues that "...it is hard to realize that most violence is not motivated by evil, greed, lust, ideology or aggression. Strange as it may seem, most violence is defensive" (Jackson 2005: 57). He suggests that the principle motivation toward violent behavior is fear—that if one does not kill, one will be killed, and that constant anxiety and vulnerability provoke extreme behavior that is really a cry for recognition denied the perpetrator by the social and political circumstances in which (usually) he finds himself. It will be clear from what I have argued so far that while this may be true up to a point—and fear is certainly a factor—actual conflict situations are much more complex than this. The perception of injustice and deprivation that comes from exclusion or non-recognition (and on that point Jackson is correct) are equally important, as is the recognition that sadism is a tragically real aspect of human psychological make-up. Ritual forms of violence such as those found in more extreme initiation ceremonies with which many of Jackson's African informants would have been familiar, occur within a known cultural context and have a conclusion when the neophytes emerge from their liminal state into a new status. But war is different—its end is not known, nor is its duration, its events are erratic and unpredictable. Its outcome may be rapid death or the slow death of endless waiting in a refugee camp, passive and dependent on events entirely outside of one's control or the largesse of distant humanitarian aid organizations. This itself points to several levels of understanding—the structural level of objective causes, the psychology of violence, and the narratives of both resentment and suffering generated by both perpetrators and victims, the process of "making sense" of the suffering inflicted or experienced, which, as I have argued elsewhere is close to the notion of "illness narratives" developed by the medical anthropologist Arthur Kleinman and the central notion in his work of understanding the "lifeworld as meaning" which help both patient and physician make sense of the illness experience as lived by the sufferer (Kleinman 1988; Clammer 2012: 165–191).

In the course of a remarkably sensitive essay relating the art of Vermeer to the Yugoslav War Crimes Tribunal, at that time sitting in The Hague, the capital of the very country in which Vermeer had created his masterpieces, the US writer Lawrence Weschler spoke with the eminent South African jurist Richard Goldstone who was then acting as the Tribunal's lead prosecutor. When asked how he envisaged the role of the Tribunal, Goldstone spoke in terms of breaking the historic cycle of vengeance inspired mayhem, since he thought that such violence is never inevitable:

> For the great majority of their histories, the Croats and Serbs and Muslims, and the Tutsis and Hutus, have lived in relative peace with one another – and they were all doing that relatively nicely once again until just recently...Such interethnic violence usually gets stoked by specific individuals intent on immediate political or material advantage, who then call forth the legacies of earlier and previously unaddressed grievances. But the guilt for the violence that results does not adhere to the entire group. Specific individuals bear the major share of the responsibility, and it is they, not the group as a whole, who need to be held to account, through a fair and meticulously detailed presentation and evaluation of evidence, precisely so that the next time around no one will be able to claim that all Serbs did this, or all Croats or all Hutus – so that people are able to see how it is specific individuals in their communities who are continually endeavoring to manipulate them in that fashion. I really believe that this is the only way the cycle can be broken. (Weschler 2005: 24)

This I think is true, but still needs to be situated in its historical and anthropological context. As social movements scholars and activists know, it is not always easy to rally people to a cause. Too much social inertia intervenes—lack of interest, other commitments, fear of entanglement in a possibly risky cause. To motivate people to involve themselves in a movement which, if evidently violent, is inherently dangerous requires the generation of a sense of grievance, of the possibility of personal gain, and the promise of excitement, adventure and the liberty to do things normally forbidden, but secretly desired. This Klaus Theweleit has shown in his detailed study of the vicious post World War 1 German *Freikorps*, founded to violently combat the rising Left in the Weimar Republic and many of whose members formed the core of the Nazi party as it rose to power. Permeated with sadism, homosexuality (since women were both desired and despised), extreme violence toward those perceived to be enemies, and drawing on the same kind of early Germanic and Teutonic mythology and symbols soon after so successfully exploited by the Nazis, the Freikorps is a paradigm case of a violent social movement, and one able to tap into deep resentments (the loss of the war, subsequent economic chaos and hyperinflation, loss of German pride) combined with the exploitation of truly pathological latent psychological tendencies, ideas of masculinity, love of uniforms and weapons and opportunities to exploit social disorganization for personal ends (Theweleit 1987, 1989).

Given this analysis, what is the way forward? I would again suggest several levels. The first is the recognition of the deep psychological forces at work in the genesis of violence, and the second is the linking of these to sociological and historical factors, while recognizing that there must be a catalyst, whether this be in the form of an event that precipitates reaction and the beginning of a cycle of violence, or of an individual. But individuals, as we have suggested, are not effective mobilizers unless they can tap into deeper real or imaginary resentments, and it is this link that lies at the basis of social movements theory (e.g. from a very large literature, Touraine 1981). A third is, drawing on the psychology of violence, the paying of much more attention to the emotions. While the body has reentered sociological and anthropological discourse in a major way in the past two decades, the sociology of the emotions is still a very underdeveloped area. Yet it is obvious that the emotions are deeply implicated in the study of conflict at every level, whether as trigger, result or sustaining energy. A fourth is the utilization of the substantial ethnographic record generated by anthropology about dispute resolution in many societies and the many effective ways that have been devised for avoiding or mediating conflict through many cultural devices ranging from talking, through poetry, the role of the elders, and concepts of the reintegration of offenders or those with grievances back into their community. Yet another is the promotion of cultures of peace, particularly through education, democratization, participation and inclusion of all stakeholders in any given society (Korostelina 2012) and the recognition that there are and can be non-violent forms of social movement (Zunes et al. 1999), and movement historically toward societies in which, while disputes will undoubtedly still occur, these will not eventuate in killing (Pim 2010; UNESCO 1997b).

At the same time these "positive" factors must be balanced by the awareness that there are new forces working toward fresh forms of social exclusion and marginalization—the effects of climate change (loss of cropland, new diseases, environmental refugees, even loss of one's country as with some of the small island states), globalization which benefits some but sidelines others and creates new categories of displacement such as low paid migrant workers, and as the leading sociologist Zygmunt Bauman has argued, the processes of modernity themselves and the loss of old categories of status and the emergence of new ones to which those without the requisite education or technological skills cannot gain entry (Bauman 2004). Conflict and the violence that it produces is thus a "moving target", and while its underlying causes may be universal, its specific manifestations will be local, rooted in particular histories, and subject to evolving political and economic regimes, environmental changes, and technological shifts, often quite outside of the power of individuals or communities to influence. And therein lies both the problem and the solution: notably autonomy or the lack of it, and the ability to exercise it and the social competence that it implies in an unhindered way. This is what lies behind the popular notion of "empowerment". But in seeking the solution to or better still avoidance of conflict that empowerment must be understood as a benign one that does not encroach on the legitimate rights of others. This should be the goal of peace education and the creation of genuine cultures of peace and mutual responsibility, and hence of holistic and just development.

References

Anderson, Benedict. 1993. *Imagined Communities: Reflections on the Origins and Spread of Nationalism*. London and New York: Verso.

Arendt, Hannah. 1970. *On Violence*. New York: Harcourt, Brace, Jovanovich.

Bauman, Zygmunt. 2004. *Wasted Lives: Modernity and Its Outcasts*. Cambridge: Polity Press.

Bax, Mart. 2004. Mass Graves, Stagnating Identification and War Violence in Rural Bosnia-Herzegovina. In *The Development of Religion/The Religion of Development*, ed. Oscar Salemink, Anton van Harskamp, and Ananta Kumar Giri, 179–190. Delft: Eburon.

Clammer, John. 2012. *Culture, Development and Social Theory: Towards an Integrated Social Development*. London and New York: Zed Books.

Clammer, John. 2015. Social Development and Peace. In *New Horizons of Human Development*, ed. A.K. Giri, 155–177. New Delhi: Studera Press.

Connerton, P. 1995. *How Societies Remember*. Cambridge: Cambridge University Press.

Cowan, J.K., M.B. Dembour, and R.A. Wilson (eds.). 2001. *Culture and Rights: Anthropological Perspectives*. Cambridge: Cambridge University Press.

Dallmayr, Fred. 2004. *Peace Talks—Who Listens?* Notre Dame, IN: Notre Dame University Press.

Daniel, Valentine. 1997. *The Anthropology of Violence: Sri Lankans, Sinhalese and Tamils*. New Delhi: Oxford University Press.

Freeman, M. 1993. *Rewriting the Self: History, Memory, Narrative*. London and New York: Routledge.

Galtung, Johan. 1975. *Essays in Peace Research*, vol. 1. Copenhagen: Christian Ejlers.

Galtung, Johan. 1990. Cultural Violence. *Journal of Peace Research* 27 (3): 291–305.

Jackson, Michael. 2005. *Existential Anthropology: Events, Exigencies and Effects*. Oxford and New York: Berghahn.

Kleinman, Arthur. 1988. *The Illness Narratives: Suffering, Healing and the Human Condition*. New York: Basic Books.

Korostelina, Karina V. (ed.). 2012. *Forming a Culture of Peace: Reframing Narratives of Intergroup Relations, Equity and Justice*. New York and Basingstoke: Palgrave Macmillan.

Kusno, Abidin. 2000. *Behind the Postcolonial: Architecture, Urban Space and Political Culture in Indonesia*. London and New York: Routledge.

Leed, Eric. 1979. *No Man's Land: Combat and Identity in World War 1*. Cambridge and New York: Cambridge University Press.

Lefebvre, Henri. 1991. *The Production of Space*. Oxford: Blackwell.

Mirzoeff, Nicholas. 2015. *How to See the World*. London: Pelican Books.

O'Brian, Jodi, and Judith A. Howard (eds.). 1998. *Everyday Inequalities: Critical Inquiries*. Oxford and Malden, MA: Blackwell.

Pim, Joam Evans (ed.). 2010. *Nonkilling Societies*. Honolulu: Center for Global Nonkilling.

Roberts, Simon. 1979. *Order and Dispute: An Introduction to Legal Anthropology*. Harmondsworth: Penguin Books.
Said, Edward W. 1985. *Orientalism*. Harmondsworth: Penguin Books.
Tal, Kali. 1996. *Worlds of Hurt: Reading the Literature of Trauma*. Cambridge and New York: Cambridge University Press.
Theweleit, Klaus. 1987. *Male Fantasies, Volume One: Women, Floods, Bodies, History*. Minneapolis: University of Minnesota Press.
Theweleit, Klaus. 1989. *Male Fantasies, Volume Two: Male Bodies: Psychoanalyzing the White Terror*. Minneapolis: University of Minnesota Press.
Touraine, Alain. 1981. *The Voice and the Eye: An Analysis of Social Movements*. Cambridge: Cambridge University Press.
UNESCO (United Nations Educational, Scientific and Cultural Organization). 1997a. *The Human Right to Peace: Declaration of the Director-General*. Paris: UNESCO.
UNESCO (United Nations Educational, Scientific and Cultural Organization). 1997b. *From a Culture of Violence to a Culture of Peace*. Paris: UNESCO.
Weschler, Lawrence. 2005. *Vermeer in Bosnia: Selected Writings*. New York: Vintage Books.
Wilson, R.A. (ed.). 1997. *Human Rights: Culture and Context. Anthropological Perspectives*. London: Pluto Press.
Yoneyama, Lisa. 1999. *Hiroshima Traces: Time, Space and the Dialectics of Memory*. Berkeley and London: University of California Press.
Young, Allen. 1997. Suffering and the Origins of Traumatic Memory. In *Social Suffering*, ed. Arthur Kleinman, Veena Das, and Margaret Lock. Berkeley and London: University of California Press.
Zunes, Stephan, Lester R. Kurtz, and Sarah Beth Asher (eds.). 1999. *Nonviolent Social Movements*. Oxford and Malden, MA: Blackwell.

CHAPTER 8

Embodying Rights

The sociology of the body has expanded in the last two decades into a major field of enquiry, with books, courses in universities, a dedicated journal (*Body and Society*) and with links to social history, the history of fashion and diet, and extending into areas that were in the past largely outside of the ambit of mainstream sociology, such as dance and performance studies. Much of this proliferating literature has emerged in the "global North" and often in the context of affluent societies where the concern with the body is not with hunger, but with diet, not with malnutrition but with body building and the construction of the "glamorized body", not with the body in physical labor, but with the body in sport and exercise. Each society of course has its "issues", and it is certainly not illegitimate for scholars of the body to be concerned with such matters as the "postmodern life-course", with fitness clubs, and with fashion. The problem is that, in the context of both globalization and multiculturalism, these are not the somatic issues that confront probably the majority of the world's population. For them, hunger, lack of clothing, health, shelter, violence inflicted on the body through conflict, displacement (as in the refugee situation), or confinement are the issues. While at first sight, the study of the body may seem to have little to do with cultural rights, closer examination shows many links, ones moreover the suggest fresh approaches to the study of rights beyond the legal language of much rights discourse.

The historical sociology of the body has thrown up many fascinating areas of investigation—the relation between religion and the body

J. Clammer, *Cultural Rights and Justice*,
https://doi.org/10.1007/978-981-13-2811-4_8

reflected in dress, dietary codes, fasting, asceticism and the encouragement of such expressive forms as dance (celebrated in India in religious contexts and for the most part denied in Europe), the whole process of what Norbert Elias has called the "civilizing process" (Elias 1978) and Stephen Mennell the "civilizing of appetite" (Mennell 1991), fashion history and the history of dance, the increasing "medicalization" of the body and the changing bodily regimes identified by Michel Foucault in relation to punishment, madness and sexuality. But as one projects these concerns into the contemporary world, it is clear that they must be supplemented by concern with the suffering and displaced body—the body in situations of drastic and unchosen (or "chosen" under political, economic or environmental duress) upheaval whether these are in the form of "natural" disasters, political displacement, war or environmental stress. This is of course the situation of the millions of refugees, political, economic or environmental, asylum seekers and exiles of various stripes, and the displacement that they experience (and with it the deprivation of culturally acceptable diet, shelter, dress and spaces for customary religious observance) constitutes the new "normal" for those in these situations.

The awareness of these all-too-common circumstances takes us beyond the narcissism of much (largely Western) sociology of the body into the consideration of the reimagining, recreation and "management" of the body under these conditions, and raises the question of the right not only to life, healthcare and shelter, but to the cultural context under which bodily expression can take place—in situations as commonplace as bathing and the notions of modesty that accompany it. If one takes the refugee situation as paradigmatic, especially in the refugee camp, the multiple forms of both physical and cultural deprivation immediately become apparent. These include of course the loss of home, familiar environment and "things"—the small items of personal value, often as containers of memory, photographs, heirlooms and poor physical conditions such as living in a tent in cold and wet weather, and attendant problems of access to sanitation and clean water. With these come crowding, forced contact with strangers, loss of privacy, physical insecurity and vulnerability to crime and exploitation. Hunger and dietary problems are common, as is what might be termed "religious deprivation"—not having any spaces to practice religion or access to ritual resources, scriptures or other necessary implements or materials—even in situations where religious succor would be a major source of strength and identity. The list can be extended even further—boredom and lack of access to any cultural resources, the expression of gender roles and sexuality under camp conditions, dependence on unknown outside agencies, profound worries about the future and the prospect of return, or if resettled, the problems of adjusting to a new culture and language, and the problem of ageing in a uprooted situation deprived quite possibly of friends and family, of respect, and of the activities consistent with one's place in the life course.

In all of these circumstances a radical reconstruction of the body image is usually entailed, whether to survive camp conditions, on resettlement in a third country, on repatriation possibly to a ruined or unrecognizable environment, on the sense of being "stuck" in a liminal situation for the long term or possibly forever, in being forced to learn a new language and culture, or, creatively, in attempting to create new forms of community whether temporary or long term in the camp or with fellow former refugees in the country of resettlement. The term "settlement" of course conceals many issues—indeed precisely those of coming to terms with a new embodiment in an alien space. The result can easily be very spoilt identities. This is particularly the case when the displaced have experienced real physical harm, torture or rape, in which normal patterns of sexuality are denied, in which elders face the prospect of ageing in a context of "futurelessness", for the disabled or less-abled in any form, where spatial boundaries are lost (for example demarcation of gendered space within the traditional house), and where youths are denied normal educational, entertainment and socialization experiences and who face another form of futurelessness, tragically providing the sources of desperation, fundamentalism and terrorism.

A common comment in such situations is that "no one listens to our stories". There are many parallels here between refugees and asylum seekers, the experiences of war veterans and disaster survivors, political and cultural exiles, the experience of statelessness, and survivors of traumas of many kinds (Tal 1996; Eyerman et al. 2013). All of this forces on us a new and expanded understanding of what the sociologist Bryan Turner has called the "somatic society" (Turner 1992), and the analysis of the three elements of body, self-identity and death, the latter signaling that the somatic is temporary and usually preceded by the numerous bodily changes that characterize ageing. The ethnocentrism of much body scholarship can be seen in the work of Chris Schilling, who, in a major work on the sociology of the body, says quite clearly that "My argument here is that, in conditions of high modernity, there is a tendency for the body to become increasingly central to the modern person's sense of self identity...The body is increasingly a phenomenon of options and choices" (Shilling 1993: 1, 3). Hence the "high modern" preoccupation with such matters as weight loss, keep-fit regimes, cosmetics, plastic surgery and of course the big spoiler—death, but then even that can be made cosmetic. The problem for the "high modern" (post-modern?) conception of the body is that while, as part of the human existential condition, the body is always vulnerable or "uncertain" in Shilling's terms, "regulating bodies" (to use Turner's phrase) become very different in circumstances of deprivation, where loss of control of the body is not simply a matter of health, ageing or the unavailability of one's favorite cosmetics, but has deep implications for identity, meaning and agency, and hence of even the possibility of cultural expression, let alone the fulfillment of one's cultural rights.

Foucault's notion of the "dominated body" has great utility here and can be extended into these typical situations of somatic deprivation. It can include for example the experience of prolonged infantalization. Long-term stigmatization, imposed and irreversible social inequalities (including loss of status in relation to previous occupation or social position), living for long periods in extreme versions of the "risk society", posing very different possibilities for "body projects" from those available to inhabitants of safe and affluent societies, and finally, the "unchosen death" far from family or familiar environment. The notion of "regulating bodies" then takes on a very different meaning when related to the actual experience and phenomenology of radical displacement. Within such a broad idea of course exist social specificities—gender, childhood, ageing, frailty, hope and the means available for the expression of emotions. Frank (1991) suggests an alternative and useful set of categories—control (how predictable the body's performance will be), desire ("whether the body is lacking or producing"), the body's relationship to others, and the self-relatedness of the body. Expanded into a more cultural frame, these can be reformulated in the context of social suffering (Kleinman et al. 1997). Such suffering can be understood to include the destabilization of established categories, the transformation of subjectivities, the recognition that there is no possibility of the "normalization" of social experience, but rather an "unappeasable experience", traumatic memory (of torture, atrocity, displacement), loss of agency, hope and expectations and political alienation such that "alienation from the political present is matched by alienation from the imagined past" (Kleinman et al. 1997: xxiii).

The situation is of course, given human resourcefulness, not all bleak. Humor, new forms of political engagement, self-management of the camps, hope embodied in possible futures of return and resettlement, the re-establishment of religious practices, education and the development of the "macho body" by young males have all been proved to be forms of adaptability. So too have been the revitalization of cultural activities—drama (Balfour 2013; Wong and Clammer 2017), dance and the revival of traditional cultural forms to address the new circumstances (Jackson and Shapiro-Phim 2008; Gough 2012), writing (the Palestinian novel and short stories for example—Rooke 1996), art and poetry (Grieder 2014). Likewise sociologically—new forms of community and networks, social, economic and political and often stretching across international boundaries aided by the cell phone, new political organizations, and the reformulation of identities despite and through the suffering body.

The Body and Cultural Rights

Cultural rights are then literally embodied: this is a condition of all cultural practices. It follows from this that the body itself has "rights"—to protection from violence and violation, to shelter, nutrition, adequate health care to ensure its preservation and well-being and the maximal possibilities for expressing itself in performance, sport, or by other means, and to culturally appropriate clothing. Such a position links the body to three other major areas of concern. One is that of food security, not only understood as the provision and guarantee of adequate nutrition in a general sense, but also ensuring that such food is likewise culturally appropriate and suitable for different age groups. The second, rarely if ever discussed in the literature on either rights, or on culture and development, is that of sexuality. Normal sexual functioning is intrinsic to life, and the deprivation of the possibility of such activity signals a major absence in the lives of many refugees and exiles. Linked to this is the denial of the possibility of a "normal" family life (accepting that this is a shifting and culturally relative category) where kinship patterns are broken, where there is little or no possibility of a cycle of maturation moving through the accepted pattern of childhood–teenage–young adult–married householder–retiree–old age. Norms governing courtship, dating, sexual activity, childbearing may be violated with little prospect of their being returned to accepted patterns in the foreseeable future. The anthropology of kinship needs to be substantially rewritten in the light of such all-too-common situations, for they are significantly different from other systemic shifts in kinship practices such as same-sex marriages, late marriage, couples living as partners rather than marrying, high divorce rates and so forth that are increasingly characteristic of affluent and stable societies rather than disrupted ones. The third, closely tied to considerations of kinship is ageing and the problems faced by the elderly when family patterns are disrupted or destroyed, and in which the ageing body experiences more and more physical challenges, often in situations where inadequate health care, nutrition and shelter are the everyday experience.

These thoughts take us back quite naturally to the issue of social suffering and the ways in which precisely *socially* induced suffering is experienced—parallel to, but on a different scale of understanding from personal illness and suffering and the "illness narratives" that individuals create to make sense of that suffering and vulnerability. The contributors to the volume cited above (Kleinman et al. 1997) note many of these features—the radical destabilization of established categories (of kinship, status, gender and more), the recognition that there will be no "normalization", but a continuous experience of displacement, traumatic memories, loss of agency, the experience of structural violence, poverty and loss of hope. The "ideal" context for the exercise of cultural rights is one of peace, stability and access to the resources that enable cultural expression. Even in the situation of globalization, where pressure is put on minority cultures in particular and there is a real danger of their erosion, documents like the UNESCO Convention tacitly assume a situation of relative cultural stability. But this is not at all the case for many: their culture may not be simply eroded by the homogenizing forces of globalization, but may be being actively attacked, or if intact to some degree, may be practiced only in the highly confining situations of conflict zones, camps or other spaces of displacement, including resettled communities in a third country where the host culture is opaque to the newly arrived, cut off from it by barriers of language, religion, diet and patterns of family life.

The suffering body is, then, central to development studies—the displacements, violence and disruptions that it so often entails acts on the bodies of those so effected. Development is not simply a matter of economics, of statistical trends, of infrastructure projects. It also acts directly and profoundly on the lives of those "developed". In cases of refugee situations and forced displacement by dams, urban redevelopment projects and the like, these somatic effects are simply magnified: in one form or another they are always there. This implies an expanded and "engaged" sociology of the body, and not merely one concerned with the narcissism of the affluent. Arthur Frank, drawing on the work of Michel Feher and collaborators (Feher et al. 1989: 12), has suggested that a fruitful approach, and one which implicitly encompasses the idea of cultural justice, lies in the project of formulating what he calls "an ethics of the body" in the context not of the exhaustion of social and cultural theory at the end of postmodernism, but rather "the beginning of a new ethical impulse to demystify domination" (Frank 1991: 39) that has fueled the rise in the later 1980s and early 1990s of such sudden interest in the human body. Among the factors that Frank identifies as stimulating this concern with the body is feminism, which, while it has its theoretical dimensions, is clearly an activist mode of thought and practice, concerned not only with analyzing the world, but also changing it. Bodies have "tasks": "Social systems may provide the context in which these tasks are defined, enacted and evaluated, but social systems themselves have no 'tasks'. The theoretical problem is to show how social systems are built up from the tasks of bodies, which then allows us to understand how bodies can experience their tasks as imposed by a system" (Frank 1991: 48).

The four dimensions of corporeal existence that Frank proposes—control (in the sense of self-control or ability to predict its own performance), desire (and the ability to fulfill desires), the body's sense of its relation to others, and the "self-relatedness" of the body (body consciousness associated with its own being, or disassociated from its own corporeality, as in some social situations and in many neurological syndromes)—all prove to be significant in the context of development or more extreme social displacements. The feeling of being dominated and without agency is damaging not only to the psyche, but also to the sense of comfortably "inhabiting" the body. The body is clearly a primary tool of communication, something that becomes most apparent when its effective use is curtailed. Frank again: "What communicative bodies are about is the capacity for recognition which is enhanced through the sharing of narratives which are fully embodied. What is shared is one body's sense of another's experience, primarily its vulnerability and suffering, but also its joy and creativity. It is when narratives are spoken from the experience of the body that they can be shared most readily.... The further narrative gets from the body of the teller, and the further the teller is from feeling at home in her or his body, the more dangerous that narrative becomes. Specifically, the more it becomes a language of appropriation. But this term takes us into our final consideration, which is how a sociology of the body can assist an ethics of the body" (Frank 1991: 89). This is, in fact, the goal—to move beyond "analytic theory" to a consideration of how bodies are to be sustained and enhanced in society, and not ground down, violated, starved, desexualized, misrepresented (as perhaps in pornography as much as in Orientalist art), appropriated, made the subject of illegitimate gaze, and generally stunted, denied or devalued. An ethics of the body is consequently an integral part of any holistic model of development and of any comprehensive theory of cultural rights. The notion of "bio-politics" popularized by Foucault and others, is not confined to spaces such as hospitals, prisons, schools and the military: its application extends to the whole of society and to modes of cultural expression of whatever form they take.

As an illustration of this, the socially activist Indian dancer Sohini Chakraborty who works with dance as a medium of healing of the bodies and psyches of survivors of sexual violence and human trafficking has rightly said, "As cycles of violence begin and end with the body, I wish, through movement, to engender freedom within these bodies, breaking the mental and emotional patterns of violence" (Chakraborty and Sarkar Munsi 2018: 240). Dance, by definition an embodied form of cultural and personal expression, demonstrates in a heightened way an "ethics of the body", as indeed do sports and other forms and other forms of expressive culture. Feminism indeed provides the leading model here, not only to patriarchal (and hence biased in favor of a particular group), but as posing key questions about the body and society, about the politics of the body, about inequalities inscribed on the body or expressed through it, often under social duress, and as a methodology for pursuing these questions rigorously.

I have argued elsewhere (Clammer 2012) that medical models also provide a useful tool for examining development and rights questions. That argument however is very different from Turner's ide of "regulating bodies" in the context of the medicalization of society. Rather it is to do with the parallel ways in which narratives are constructed by sufferers from illness and the often unwilling recipients of "development". Both try to make sense of the experience not so much in scientific terms, but in constructing patterns of meaning and trying to make sense of why this particular set of unsought events is happening to their particular bodies and how those effects, possibly quite drastic ones, are effecting their relationship both to their own bodies and to those of others. The *experience* itself then becomes the center of attention, however much or little of the structural factors that have induced the condition are understood. Indeed, for most humans at some point in their lives, such an experience is virtually unavoidable. As David Morris puts it in his book on contemporary illness "Unlike robots or rabbits, humans possess a tendency towards repeated and often protracted illnesses that seem finally less a fatal flaw in our design than a mysterious signature" (Morris 1998: 1). Speaking of the subsequent chapters in their book on social suffering, Kleinman, Das and Lock say the following:

> The authors discuss why a language of dismay, disappointment, bereavement and alarm that sounds not at all like the usual terminology of policy and programs may offer a more valid means for Describing what is at stake in human experiences of political catastrophe and social structural violence, for professionals as much as for victims/perpetrators, and may also make better sense of how the clash among globalizing discourses and localized social realities so often ends up prolonging personal and collective tragedy. (Kleinman et al. 1997: xi)

Tied up with such suffering is also the question of memory, whether of atrocities inflicted on one's own body, or witnessed being inflicted on others, or of nostalgia, memories real or imagined of the golden and tranquil life before conflict and displacement. As Valentine Daniel shows in his study of Tamil victims of violence in Sri Lanka, when even photographs of the dead or disappeared have faded or become lost, the survivors often retreated into silence (Daniel 1997). But that silence was not one of healing, for the cognitive, affective and ontological qualities of the survivors of trauma persists, and perhaps may never be eradicated (Young 1997). The body is the deposit of memory, and the neurology of pain ensures that while suffering may be cognitively suppressed, it remains, deeply transcribed into the tissues and muscles. That is precisely why so many body techniques (Rolfing, Reiki, forms of massage, dance and movement therapies, the Reich method and many others) have as their basis the idea that the traumas of memory are encoded into the muscles of the body and only with their physical release can the memories be healed or managed.

Embodiment and the Politics of Recognition

Referring to Charles Taylor's concept of the 'politics of recognition' in the context of multicultural societies (Taylor 1994), Dipesh Chakrabarty notes that "misrecognition shows not just a lack of due respect. It can inflict a grievous wound" (Chakrabarty 2011: 21). Such wounds are not only historical, the context in which they are usually understood, but equally misrepresentations of the body, again a subject central to dance scholarship and to the "body status" of dancers—as feminized, as subjects of a sexualized gaze and courtesans rather than as genuine performers, as outcasts and as other denigrated roles (e.g. Chatterjee 1990; Morcom 2014). The misrecognition and exclusion of any social group, be it an ethnic minority, a religious one, or the practitioners of a way of life or art not accepted by the mainstream, has similar structural characteristics, and all are "inscribed on the body" as the many studies of Dalits or "untouchables" have so clearly shown. What can be worn, whether one may cross the road in front of a Hindu temple, let alone actually enter it, whether one can take water from a common well or pond, whether one can give or accept food from another, whether one's cultural expressions are respected: all these and more are expressions of this bodily inscription. The body is thus the basis for all sociocultural organization and so any form of cultural analysis must start from the phenomenology of the body.

While the sociology of the body of course accepts this—it is obviously the rationale for the whole sub-discipline—it is certainly not evident that it has for the most part either considered the suffering body as its central theme, or, by extension, the role of bodies in relation to development processes on the one hand, and rights on the other. The notion propagated by Shilling quoted above, that "My argument here is that, in conditions of high modernity, there is a tendency for the body to become increasingly central to the modern person's sense of self-identity" (Shilling 1993: 1) in which it is only the unfortunate fact of death that interferes with this narcissistic identification, is, at best, ironic when read in the light of such issues as poverty, untouchability, displacement, asylum, war (civil and otherwise), terrorism, racism, sexism and ageism. The title of his book is *The Body and Social Theory*, clearly in the light of the aforementioned, is a deeply ethnocentric and limited one, one limited in fact to a possible theorization of a minority—the affluent—even in "advanced" or "developed" societies. In fact, the whole model needs to be reconstructed by reformulating the basic analytical issues—diet, agency, the "management" of the body, stigmas and so forth, in the context of the mass suffering of the body. The closest that Shilling comes to this is to introduce a number of (Western, English- speaking) writers who have touched on the construction of the gendered body and the embodiment of inequality in such contexts. In his work on "regulating bodies" Bryan Turner comes a little closer (Turner 1992), but almost wholly in the situation of the medicalization of the body in which human frailty has to be taken into consideration.

One of the most fruitful ways to examine the alternative possibility of a focus on the vulnerable body is to explore the literature that deals with situations of unchosen physical extremity—concentration camps, forced labor, conflict zones, torture and the deliberate infliction of suffering through starvation or sub-standard living conditions on prisoners of war, refugees or populations singled out for persecution. Sadly of course, many such examples exist, whether historical ones such as the Jewish and Armenian Holocausts, the vicious Belgian regime in the Congo. The decimation of the Cambodian population under Pol Pot and the Khmer Rouge regime, civilian populations in the civil war in Sierra Leone, Somalia and other conflict zones in Africa, and contemporary ones—civilians caught in the war zones of Syria, in the areas controlled during their thankfully brief ascendency by the "Islamic State", Tibetan refugees living out their lives in India, asylum seekers making the dangerous crossing of the Mediterranean in the hope of reaching a safe haven in Europe. All of these cases and many more illustrate all too clearly how suffering is "inscribed" on the body, and how, while not so much studied, the subsequent process of "normalization", insofar as it can ever be achieved or recovered, involves bodywork of a profound kind: the reconceptualization of one's own body in the light of radically new circumstances of Being. The issues here are in fact ones of Ontology—of creating new phenomenologies of the body where the old ones and the taken for granted ones fail. For some, this can be a chosen experience—by exploring new possibilities for one's body through dance, meditation or some other bodily technique. But for many others it is an unchosen reality, one perhaps analogous to the experience of someone who has lost a limb or a faculty such a sight or hearing: the necessity to live in a new form in a world rendered unfamiliar, yet in which it is still necessary to navigate. This once again takes us back to the issue of rights—the right to free bodily expression, and the right to a "model" of the body and its presentation and "wrapping" considered appropriate to the culture in question. Rights are literally embodied, and must be protected as such.

Performing Rights

Rights in the abstract are simply legal marks on paper. To be realized they have to be enacted. Like ethnicity (Clammer 2015), and gender (Butler 1993), culture too has to be performed for it to be realized. This recognition renders rights dynamic and not so much something to be discussed in the abstract as rendered transparent through performance. They need to be expressed to be real, except in a purely formal and legalistic sense. This is not only a general and perhaps fairly obvious point, but it also links the performance of rights both to the body (the vehicle of expression), and to performance in the sense of theatre, dance, music, mime, puppetry and the other concrete expressions of culture. The preservation of cultural diversity often actually means the preservation of exactly those forms, forms which embody the culture in question, as do its architecture, visual arts, religion, dress, language and crafts. The manifestations of cultural rights are thus very visible and not at all mysterious. But even as there is an "ethics of the body", so too there is an ethics of performance: the requirement for performance to be authentic in terms of the culture that it embodies and expresses, and for it to be included within the "politics of recognition"—respected that is as the culture in action (Read 1993; see also Rae 2009). If the body is politicized, it too can effect politics, and perhaps move it in a more humane direction, one that respects the dignity and vulnerability of the body and respects its boundaries and expressive needs, and which accepts the human mortality of the potential oppressor as much as the victim. Any worthwhile utopia (for a contemporary example see Callenbach 2004) assumes or creates a methodology for the transformation of the body, as it must, the body being the only vehicle of the new society unless we be spirits.

This is reflected in the ideas of individuals whose work falls far outside the scope of conventional rights discourse and conventional development discourse. Speaking of the prominent South Indian dancer Chandralekha, the theatre and cultural critic (and theatrical producer) Rustom Bharucha says "The body, Chandra believes, is our only defense against negative forces in our society. Only if we are in touch with our inner energies can we control our position in this world" (Bharucha

1993). The German theatre scholar Erika Fischer-Lichte has likewise argued for the transformative power of performance—its ability to recover the sensations of life, to re-enchant, to reveal, to build communities (even if only transitory ones), and as she argues following the work of the anthropologist Thomas Csordas (1994) that culture is grounded in the body, or as Csordas himself puts it, embodiment is the "existential ground of culture and the self" (Csordas 1994: 6; Fischer-Lichte 2008). This being so, rights too must be rooted in the body, and respect for the body as the vehicle of both culture and the self.

References

Balfour, Michael (ed.). 2013. *Refugee Performance: Practical Encounters.* Bristol: Intellect.

Bharucha, Rustom. 1993. *Theatre and the World: Performance and the Politics of Culture.* London and New York: Routledge.

Butler, Judith. 1993. *Bodies That Matter: On the Discursive Limits of 'Sex'.* New York: Routledge.

Callenbach, Ernest. 2004. *Ecotopia.* Berkeley: Banyan Tree Books.

Chakrabarty, Dipesh. 2011. History and the Politics of Recognition. In *Theorizing the Present: Essays for Partha Chatterjee*, ed. Anjan Ghosh, Tapati Guha-Thakurta, and Janaki Nair, 21–34. New Delhi: Oxford University Press.

Chakraborty, Aishika, and Urmimala Sarkar Munsi. 2018. Moving with a Purpose: Women Dancers in Dialogue with Empowerment, Rehabilitation and Therapy. In *The Moving Space: Women in Dance*, ed. Urmimala Sarkar Munsi and Aishika Chakraborty, 238–263. New Delhi: Primus Books.

Chatterjee, Ratnabali. 1990. *From the Karkhana to the Studio: Changing Roles of Patrons and Artists in Bengal.* New Delhi: Books and Books.

Clammer, John. 2012. *Culture, Development and Social Theory: Towards an Integrated Social Development.* London and New York: Zed Books.

Clammer, John. 2015. Performing Ethnicity: Performance, Gender, Body and Belief in the Construction and Signaling of Identity. *Ethnic and Racial Studies Review* 38 (13): 2159–2166.

Csordas, Thomas (ed.). 1994. *Embodiment and Experience: The Existential Ground of Culture and Self.* Cambridge: Cambridge University Press.

Daniel, Valentine E. 1997. *The Anthropology of Violence: Sri Lankans, Sinhalese and Tamils.* New Delhi: Oxford University Press.

Elias, Norbert. 1978. *The Civilizing Process, Vol. 1: The History of Manners.* Oxford: Basil Blackwell.

Eyerman, Ron, Jeffrey C. Alexander, and Elizabeth Butler Breese. 2013. *Narrating Trauma: On the Impact of Collective Suffering.* London and New York: Paradigm Publishers.

Feher, Michael, Ramona Naddaff, and Nadia Tazi. 1989. *Fragments for a History of the Human Body, Part One*. New York: Zone.

Fischer-Lichte, Erika. 2008. *The Transformative Power of Performance: A New Aesthetic*, trans. Saskya Iris Jain. London and New York: Routledge.

Frank, Arthur W. 1991. For a Sociology of the Body: An Analytical Review. In *The Body: Social Process and Cultural Theory*, ed. Mike Featherstone, Mike Hepworth, and Bryan S. Turner, 36–102. London and Newbury Park: Sage.

Gough, Kathleen M. 2012. Natural Disaster, Cultural Memory: Montserrat Adrift in the Black and Green Atlantic. In *Readings in Performance and Ecology*, ed. Wendy Arons and Theresa J. May, 101–112. London and New York: Palgrave Macmillan.

Grieder, Andrea. 2014. Rwanda: Healing and the Aesthetics of Poetry. In *Arts and Aesthetics in a Globalizing World*, ed. Raminder Kaur and Parul Dave-Mukherji, 135–151. London: Bloomsbury.

Jackson, Naomi, and Toni Shapiro-Phim (eds.). 2008. *Dance, Human Rights, and Social Justice: Dignity in Motion*. Lanham, MD: Scarecrow Press.

Kleinman, Arthur, Veena Das, and Margaret Lock (eds.). 1997. *Social Suffering*. Berkeley and London: University of California Press.

Mennell, Stephen. 1991. On the Civilizing of Appetite. In *The Body: Social Process and Cultural Theory*, ed. Mike Featherstone, Mike Hepworth, and Bryan S. Turner, 126–156. London and Newbury Park: Sage.

Morcom, Anna. 2014. *The Illicit World of Indian Dance: Cultures of Exclusion*. New York: Oxford University Press.

Morris, David B. 1998. *Illness and Culture in the Postmodern Age*. Berkeley and London: University of California Press.

Rae, Paul. 2009. *Theatre and Human Rights*. New York and Basingstoke: Palgrave Macmillan.

Read, Allen. 1993. *Theatre and Everyday Life: An Ethics of Performance*. London: Routledge.

Rooke, Tetz. 1996. The Most Important Thing Is What Happens Inside Us: Personal Identity in Palestinian Autobiography. In *Identity in Asian Literature*, ed. Lisbeth Littrup, 231–235. Richmond: Curzon Press for the Nordic Institute of Asian Studies.

Shilling, Chris. 1993. *The Body and Social Theory*. London and Newbury Park: Sage.

Tal, Kali. 1996. *Worlds of Hurt: Reading the Literature of Trauma*. New York and Cambridge: Cambridge University Press.

Taylor, Charles. 1994. The Politics of Recognition. In *Multiculturalism*, ed. Amy Gutman. Princeton: Princeton University Press.

Turner, Bryan S. 1992. *Regulating Bodies: Essays in Medical Sociology*. London and New York: Routledge.

Wong, Pearly, and John Clammer. 2017. Performance and Development: Theatre for Social Change. In *The Aesthetics of Development: Art, Culture and Social Transformation*, ed. John Clammer and A.K. Giri, 291–308. New York and Basingstoke: Palgrave Macmillan.

Young, Allen. 1997. Suffering and the Origins of Traumatic Memory. In *Social Suffering*, ed. Arthur Kleinman, Veena Das, and Margaret Lock, 245–260. Berkeley and London: University of California Press.

CHAPTER 9

Transformative Narratives of Peace and Justice

Despite efforts by the United Nations, many NGOs and civil society organizations, peace still eludes our shared world, a subject explored in Chapter 7. Many deeply well-meaning (and in some cases effective) initiatives have been attempted to end war and conflict and to seek lasting peace on our planet. Yet we are evidently and sadly far from that goal, a situation that suggests that fresh approaches should be tried. At the very least, whether fully effective or not, they might add to the vocabulary of possibilities available to us. Key to the idea that I will explore here is this notion of "narrative"—the stories that individuals and cultures create to explain their perceived place in the world, to structure their memories, to relate themselves to nature, to organize their imaginative lives and to formulate images of the future, whether that future be one of anticipation and hope, or of fear and uncertainty. Culture itself can be thought of as a kind of narrative—the "metastory" which a group of people have evolved as the key to their identity and place in the world—and so the stories that they tell of past, present and future are the indicators and symptoms of how they place themselves in relation to others (human and otherwise), the cosmos and their desired way of life—the utopia as it were that lies hidden in the myths of all cultures and the deep levels of their collective psyche.

Of course stories are not the whole story. Any fundamental conception of and practice of, peace, must be rooted in social justice and "development"—the provision of adequate levels of livelihood, health, freedom, safety, leisure, and the possibility of self-expression (the arts),

J. Clammer, *Cultural Rights and Justice*,
https://doi.org/10.1007/978-981-13-2811-4_9

equity, autonomy both within a given society and between it and its neighbors (Clammer 2015b). Without these, all stories will speak bitterness. But even then, crucial to social health is *voice*—the ability to tell one's story and to have others listen, and in an ideal situation, to respond, something indeed very like the idea of communicative justice built into Jurgen Habermas' idea of communicative action as defining the nature of social inter-action. My emphasis here will be on voice, and specifically on the ways in which narratives can not only reflect current reality, but also have huge potential as transformative agents toward lasting peace, justice and equity. The social critic and critic of corporate-led globalization David Korten has rightly argued that "To create a just, sustainable, and compassionate post-corporate world we must face up to the need to create a new core culture, a new political center, and a new economic mainstream" in order to bring about "a new integral culture that affirms life in all its dimensions" (Korten 1999: 261)—a model in which new cultural forms are paramount. In a later work he expands on this by suggesting that to do this we must create "new stories" in order to redirect our civilization (if such it be) away from "Empire"—patterns of exploitation, hierarchy and domination, to "Earth Community"—a culture based on partnership, cooperation, sharing, social justice and a harmonious relationship to the rest of nature, of which we are clearly (and a dangerously destructive) part, a phenomenon that he calls the "Great Turning" (Korten 2006). Let us then turn to exploring this fertile possibility.

Narratives of Hope

Let us start, a little unusually perhaps, with a quotation from a poem, one by the leading American poet Wendell Berry, whose poetry is especially interesting as he is also and has long been, a practicing farmer, who in one of his works makes the poignant point that "For want of songs and stories they have dug away the soil, paved over what is left… so that the good that was there cannot be called back/except by long waiting, by great sorrow" (Berry 2012: 317). The distinguished British poet W.H. Auden famously stated that "poetry makes nothing happen". Often the quotation ends there, but in fact Auden went on to say ".....it survives/ In the valley of its sayings where executives/Would never want to tamper; it flows south/From ranches of isolation and the busy griefs,/ Raw towns that we believe and die in; it survives/A way of happening, a mouth" (Auden 1972: 82). Wendell Berry would clearly agree, and the whole thrust of this paper is that Auden was correct: poetry (and narratives in general) can make very much happen. Stories do make a difference and this is true at many levels. Our whole world is constructed through narratives—science itself and not only literature, written or oral, is an example of a currently dominating narrative or set of narratives—that have immensely powerful effects on how we view our place in the universe (and even that there *is* a universe within which to see ourselves). Stories structure our experience, whether delivered to us through oral forms, the written word, film, radio, the visual or performing arts, and whether in the form of literature, science, non-fiction accounts of the world, representations embodied in art or film, advertising or propaganda. The nature and quality of those stories is consequently crucial. The trivial trivializes, the untruth falsifies, the beautiful and imaginative inspire. They are powerful in a way that no other medium is when they touch the deep wellsprings of emotion and spirit, but dangerously disenchanting when shallow and encouraging of forms of behavior that are ultimately anti-social, unhealthy or damaging the environment. They can also lose their power if not renewed, as the tired language of much of the old Left or traditional religion has experienced when they find that people are simply no longer listening.

There are important parallels between the role of narratives in medicine and illness and in relation to peace as can be seen if we substitute that word for "illness" in narratives where bodily dysfunction is tragically present. In discussing the diaries of the critic Anatole Broyard who created a narrative around his own terminal prostate cancer, David Morris notes that "He emphasizes that narrative contains or releases therapeutic powers. A sick person, he contends, can make a story out of illness as a way of trying to 'detoxify' it". In seeking to detoxify his own illness, Broyard experiments with inventing 'mini-narratives' and exploring the resources of metaphor: 'I saw my illness as a visit to a disturbed country… I imagined it as a love affair with a demented woman who demanded things I had never done before' (Morris 1998: 45). Stories, Morris suggests, are what he calls 'anti-bodies against illness and pain', in which the patient is 'no longer a victim of disease, not the object of medicine, but a person struggling to recover and reshape the voice that illness so often takes from us' (Morris 1998: 48). Morris, in his study if illness, places narrative at the heart of responses to human distress:

> The social, cultural and personal dimensions of illness must be understood through other means, and one neglected but useful source is narrative. Narrative, we might say, constitutes a mode of understanding appropriate for situations too variable and too untidy for laboratory analysis. Furthermore, storytellers thrive at the margins of power, casting a skeptical eye on contemporary culture, and their somewhat independent status permits them to offer impassioned critiques, visionary alternatives, and an outsider's objectivity. Narrative may also require readers to confront self-consciously the ways in which their culture has taught them to think about illness, to imagine ways in which they might experience a healthier relation to the earth...We need a knowledge that comes with narrative. (Morris 1998: 89)

Translating such an approach into the consideration of peace (and non-peace is after all a kind of illness) points us toward a fresh methodology for rethinking peace studies, since it shifts the emphasis from external factors to the ways in which peace and conflict is internalized, expressed and interacts with the subjectivities of its agents, including, in situations of conflict, both victims and perpetrators, those at the roots of conflict and those suffering from it. The pursuit of peace is not merely an activity of "professionals" or "experts", but is at the heart of the existential experience of all humans and non-human creatures. Whatever its sources, "social suffering ruins the collective and intersubjective connections of experience and gravely damages subjectivity" (Kleinman et al. 1997: x).

In other words, the objective and structural conditions of peace/non-peace need to be balanced by two other important elements: the stories that individuals tell to make sense of the trauma and stress that they may experience as (damaged) social actors, and the cultural soil out of which these arise. The latter is important for two reasons—one is that the nature of stories themselves varies with culture and with the historical experience, religion, myths and notions of identity prevalent in any given example, and the other is the fact that, like "social suffering", non-peace arises out of our cultures and civilizations themselves. Conflict does not just appear from no-where: it is a product of our culture, as are the other non-sustainable aspects of our current planetary civilization (Clammer 2016). It is at the point where life-worlds and the structural characteristics of economy and politics intersect that narratives arise. The need to encourage, affirm and act on stories is part of the process that Kleinman calls "remoralization"—the empowerment of subjects through helping subjects subject to wrenching changes to redefine their place in the world of meanings and social networks disrupted by conflict and trauma. At this point the relationship between memories and narratives becomes significant. Studies in the sociology of trauma (e.g. Clammer 2012: 192–219) have shown clearly how the understandable emphasis on memory, and keeping memories alive, among survivors or relatives of victims of violence can also perpetuate cycles of revenge, hatred and almost permanent conflict. This has been clearly seen in the Balkans, where ancient conflicts and the telling of endless stories that keep them alive, still poison the lives of the currently living. As we saw in Chapter 7, in his chilling essay, Mart Bax discusses the destruction of a monument to Cetnik (Serbian) victims of Croat partisans during World War 2 by contemporary Croat nationalists in the village of Surmanci, who commented on this destruction to the author that their motive was clear "We killed the dead because they kept them alive" (Bax 2004: 180), an event that Bax glosses as the ultimate form of ethnic cleansing. While memorials to the past are commonplace, positive images of the future are rare. This is unfortunate, as violence feeds on itself through its "mythologization"—the constant invocation of past wars, crimes, atrocities, on the part not necessarily of victims, but of their descendants who may have experienced no such thing, but keep that past alive through stories, including of who qualifies as a "hero" (a very loaded and significant category of culture). Any acquaintance with "popular culture" immediately reinforces this perception, the amount of violence contained in films, comics, video-games and available on demand by way of the Internet is amazing in any culture that professes itself to be committed to peace.

A fundamental question then arises: "Why in the process of seeking human freedom, happiness and fulfillment are violence and suffering assumed? Are there not other models through which we might pursue social justice, harmony with nature and the expansion of creativity?" (Clammer 2012: 218–219). The search for the answer to this should lie at the heart of social and cultural theory and practice. The answer, I am suggesting here, lies in culture itself. If we can agree that our current planetary crisis and its many inter-locking dimensions (violence, poverty, climate change, species loss, and yet others), arises from culture: blindness to certain major problems which will have and are already having unimaginable impacts such as climate change (Ghosh 2016; Klein 2014), our destructive willingness to continue to pursue path-dependent patterns knowing that they will almost certainly end in disaster, our penchant for wars rather than negotiation as a solution to disputes, our cultural love of violence expressed in many sports and our "entertainment" choices, our toleration of perfectly obvious inequalities and injustices (racism, sexism, ageism, poverty) that are usually well within the reach of positive social intervention, our building of a vast and complex economy that works to favor the few at the expense of many and of the environment, our dysfunctional politics, and no doubt even more. But the paradox of culture is that while it is in many cases the source of our problems, by the same token many of the solutions also lie within it. This of course has been the master theme of the magisterial work of Roberto Mangabeira Unger: that while social structures do indeed constrain, they are not set in concrete, that society is in a constant state of becoming, and can be changed, and that social alternatives arise from the imagination (Unger 2001). If the latter claim is true, then it is through the imagination that the future will be shaped. There is then no "there is no alternative" position if we will not allow it.

But there is an important corollary to this: that the world has changed in fundamental and irreversible ways, and so that imagination cannot be directed at simply repeating or dusting off old models or recovering "tradition", which as we now well know is or was often invented itself. This is not to reject the past or the importance of memory: it is to place them in a new context, one in which a new future has to be shaped, drawing certainly on the past, but with its essential orientation to an emerging temporality which has no precedents and therefore cannot be either interpreted or "managed" on the basis of old techniques inherited from that past. Climate change for example on its current scale and humanly caused will intersect with many issues—agriculture, resources, poverty—and hence with peace, since likely future conflicts are much more likely to be fueled by these factors than by the old geopolitical ones of the past. So let us think seriously what this means. If the world that we knew is already gone, then we must make a new one or live in the decaying ruins of the old. Bill McKibben argued now almost twenty years ago that "nature" as we once knew it is gone—there is no pristine wilderness left untouched to some degree by human activities (McKibben 1989). Forests are effected by industrially produced acid rain, the oceans are full of plastic even in their most remote regions and at considerable depths, vast areas of the Earth have been transformed by industrial agriculture, our meat is full of anti-biotics fed to animals to protect them from diseases induced by their over-crowding and unsanitary living conditions on "feedlots" not farms, and our vegetables infested with pesticides and chemical fertilizer residues. Languages and the indigenous wisdom that they embody are being lost at the same rate as biodiversity loss is occurring. If we wish seriously to reshape this profoundly altered world, then new imaginative means are required, even more so than new technologies or techniques.

Narratives of Peace

If we then turn our attention to the relationship between narratives and peace, where does this take us? The simple answer (although perhaps more complex in practice) is the creation of new stories. What are the possible sources for such stories? Firstly, the spiritual traditions of a given culture. Without fail, these point to an ideal world—one in which the lion lies down with the lamb, and which justice is the norm not the exception. Whether conceived in terms of paradise, a renewed Earth, a perpetual garden or as a social and economic utopia, such "models" are far from being merely fantasies, but rather reveal deep longings. Such longings are also embodied in many cases in myth, stories of creation being also frequently account of how, at the beginning of things, such conditions of perfection did indeed exist. A second source is in the traditional relationship of a culture to the Earth. Almost all cultures, however much they might violate it in practice, have what we might term an "Earth ethic"—an understanding of the symbiotic relationship between humans and their societies and the larger biosphere. In Japanese and in many Middle Eastern cultures, and of course in the early Biblical accounts of creation, it is the garden which provides the image of the ideal environment—a remarkable balance in successful cases of nature and human creativity, and one endorsed by recent studies in landscape art of the kind of ideal environment that most people choose when given a range of choices. Thirdly, all cultures have ideals of social justice, often tied in with a larger cosmology. The Biblical book of Isaiah for example is one of the most subversive and radical documents yet produced by human beings, and roots strong ideals of social justice in a context of people's relationship to the land, to ethics and to a particular Hebraic conception of the nature of the spiritual universe. Fourthly there is what the major but rather neglected German social theorist Ernst Bloch called "the principle of hope"—the fact that we are a forward-looking species and anticipate as well as remember. Literature, the embodiment of many of our narratives, reflects this, especially in the genres known as fantasy or science fiction. As suggested above, a key to understanding how a culture thinks about itself and how it thinks about peace, is to look at its conception of the hero—as a figure of violence, or one of justice seeking? a warrior or cultivator? a spiritual figure or a destroyer? The situation of the planet today clearly calls for new concepts of heroism.

Many of the institutions of our culture are implicated in generating narratives that either contribute to peace or work against it, in particular those of the media and education. The media through its various branches—television, film, newspapers, magazines, advertising—has a profound effect on the formation of subjectivities: our understandings of ourselves, others, the world, our choice of life paths including careers, our understanding of the Earth, so without changing the content and purpose of the media only distorted and even destructive stories can emerge. The same is true of education, which, we might suggest, should not only contain "peace education", but that all education should be about peace. For example, in his book *Transformative Learning* the Canadian educationalist Edmund O'Sullivan (O'Sullivan 1999) has offered a developed vision for the recovery of what he calls an "Ecozoic" vision as the basis for education. This vision includes the ideas of teaching cosmology ("Big History" as some are calling it) as the context of all human life, of critiquing what he calls the "dream structure" of (initially largely Western) conceptions of the world—ideas such as growth, progress, development, power, consumption, competition, patriarchy, war and class—and proposing an alternative based on education for justice, Earth awareness, peace, diversity and creativity, and which sees the correct approach to existence as a mystery to be savored, not set of technical problems to be "mastered" or "managed". Many of these ideas are now encapsulated in the popular idea of sustainability, a notion which in its fullest expression, should go well beyond survival, to a vision of an abundant life (Clammer 2016). The notion of creativity is very important here, suggesting that the arts in their various manifestations should be at the heart of education and not at the periphery as is usually the case. Art itself is in many ways "utopian"—it offers alternative visions (quite literally) and stimulates the imagination, and imagination cannot be confined, but can spill over into many areas, from art into the "social imagination" for example, and indeed historically, many social movements have been preceded by or accompanied by, cultural and artistic movements: the two are rarely separate.

Today, all media, including the so-called "social media" are capable of generating new narratives, and some have successfully done so, such as the blockbuster movie *Avatar* with its anti-racist, anti-colonial and pro-nature story. Theatre has long had a distinguished record of creating and performing new stories, for through it, as the distinguished promoter of "applied theatre" and a number of movements that have arisen from it (including the ideas of an "aesthetics of the oppressed" and a "poetics of the oppressed"), Augusto Boal put it (ideas which have found echoes in so-called "Third Cinema"—such as that of a "Cinema of Hunger"): "We are discovering ourselves. Above all that we are discovering that we can change ourselves and change our world" (Boal 2008: ix). There are many "By-products" of the recovery and reinvention of narratives of peace, which include the rerooting of the local in an era when indigenous cultures and their languages are disappearing yet have coded into them vast amounts of social, ecological, agricultural, medical and spiritual knowledge which, once lost, is lost forever as a living tradition, the linking of cultural action and poetics, as exemplified in the works of leading Latin American poets such as Pablo Neruda and Octavio Paz, and of East European ones such as Czeslaw Milosz, the "re-enchantment" of an increasingly disenchanted world, and the promotion of the unity of the arts—for example music and poetry, or as the African singer Angelique Kidjo (who cannot read music, but like traditional singers, memorizes and composes by ear) has aptly put it "An artist's role is not to ignite violence. You ignite peace" (quoted in Parales 2014: 17; see also Clammer 2015a: 101–120). The North American poet Alison Hawthorne Deming has nicely summed up these aspects of art.

Art can serve activism by teaching an attentiveness to existence and by enriching the culture in which our roots are set down. Culture is both the crop we grow and the soil in which we grow it. And human culture is the most powerful evolutionary force on Earth these days. The grief we feel at abuses of human power is the first step toward transforming that power for good. Legislation, information and instruction cannot effect change at this emotional level—although they play a significant role. Art is necessary because it gives us a new way of thinking and speaking, shows us what we are and what we have been blind to, and gives us new language and forms in which to see ourselves. To effect profound cultural change requires that we educate ourselves about our own interior wildness that has led us into such a hostile relationship with the forces that sustain us. Work on the self is work on the culture (Deming 2001: 68).

This view is echoed by the major Italian novelist Italo Calvino who rightly says "Literature is necessary to politics above all when it gives voice to whatever is without a voice, when it gives a name to what as yet has no name, especially to what the language of politics excludes or attempts to exclude…Literature is like an ear that can hear things beyond the understanding of the language of politics; it is like an eye that can see beyond the color spectrum perceived by politics" (Calvino 1986: 98).

Narratives then can be conservative; they can also be subversive. This idea is at the center of Unger's thinking: "The developed conception of an alternative, promising a way to realize more fully our interests and ideas, puts the will on the side of the imagination. The illusions of false necessity arise because we surrender to the social world, and then begin to mistake present society for possible humanity, giving into the ideas and attitudes that make the established order seem natural, necessary or authoritative" (Unger 2001: xx). These ideas help us to refurbish the concept and role of the prophet—perhaps now as much a secular figure as a religious one. Or as the Biblical scholar Walter Brueggemann phrases it: "In offering symbols the prophet has two tasks. One is to mine the memory of this people and to educate them to use the tools of hope. The other is to recognize how singularly words, speech, language and phrase shape consciousness and define reality. The prophet is the one who, by the use of these tools of hope, contradicts the presumed world of the kings, showing both that the presumed world does not square with the facts and that we have been taught a lie and have believed because the people with the hardware and the printing press told us it was that way" (Brueggemann 1988: 66). And one of these tools is "futuring fantasy", for as the very prophetic Sufi poet Jelaluddin Rumi long ago put it "The world of phantasy is broader than the world of concepts. For all concepts are born in phantasy. The world of phantasy likewise is narrow in relation to the world out of which fantasy comes into being" (Arberry 1994: 202). Or as a more recent poet Octavio Paz rephrased it "Imagination: a faculty of our nature to change itself" (Paz 1990: 78). The role of the poet, or any generator of new narratives, is thus, not necessarily, to directly engage in politics, but to reclaim the imagination, through which politics itself will in turn be reclaimed. When the leading German-Jewish philosopher and social theorist Hannah Arendt was asked whether she thought that storytelling made any difference or contribute to promoting positive and humane political and social change, she answered firmly in the affirmative.

Compared with the reality that comes from being seen and heard, even the greatest forces of intimate life—the passions of the heart, the thoughts of the mind, the delights of the senses—lead an uncertain, shadowy kind of existence unless and until they are transformed, deprivatized and deindividualized, as it were, into a shape to fit them for public appearance. The most current of such transformations occurs in storytelling…Each time we talk about things that can be experienced only in privacy or intimacy, we bring them out into a sphere where they will assume a kind of reality which, their intensity notwithstanding, they never could have had before (Arendt 1958: 179–180).

Stories then have power—to link the internal and the external, and above all to redefine through the imagination, the world that we want to see and create. The power to narrate (and to suppress other narratives as every despot and colonialist knows all too well) is not a minor thing, a mere "literary" activity: it is the power to shape, and thus to transform. As the scholar of narratives Hanna Meretoja has clearly put it, storytelling is at the basis of the most fundamental ways that we structure our worlds and learn how to behave within them (Meretoja 2018).

New World/New Stories

If indeed it is true that the world we have known and long assumed to be permanent is gone and cannot be recovered except through memory and nostalgia, then new stories are necessary. The cutting edge of art should not then be clever new techniques, but the ability to write and visualize not only what is, but also what might be. This should take us beyond the trivial and even poisonous stories and imagination that infest our "popular culture" and reflect communal fantasies no longer possible, or if possible, at huge expense to the environment and other human beings (many forms of "growth", "progress" and "development" fall into this category), As we enter a profoundly altered world, old experiences are no longer a reliable guide to the future. As the Australian critic James Bradley notes in writing paradoxically about the lack of writing addressing the massive consequences of climate change (Bradley 2017), that the current upsurge of books, fiction and largely non-fiction, about nature, and to a lesser extent the re-emergence of fantasy literature (both science fiction and what may presumably be called the "Harry Potter" phenomenon not discussed by Bradley) signals not just a reaction to the climate crisis, but also new forms of narrative that are beginning to grapple with it, including in new imaginative forms. Not least this new surge of nature writing to some extent decenters the human and places us, correctly, not as the masters of nature, but simply as one of its (dangerously sophisticated) manifestations. Linking this to a burgeoning environmental movement, including such significant subsections as "Deep Ecology", a significant shift in narrative paradigms may well be (if rather belatedly) under way. Such narratives must necessarily cross the bridge between the personal and the political. Late capitalist globalization, the regime under which virtually all of us live, has unhinged social relations, undermined communities and civic institutions, attacked the environment, and led to the situation long ago described by Karl Marx as that in which "all that is solid melts into air". The new stories, particularly those that relate to peace in its broadest sense, cannot be simply escapist, but must engage themselves creatively with the forces that have brought us to our present impasse, and with the possible routes that lead out of the dark valley into, as far as we can humanly achieve it, those sunlit highlands of which so much utopian literature speaks.

This possibility is beautifully illustrated in practice by the work on the anthropologist and poet Andrea Grieder in her work with poetry as healing in Rwanda, a country that has been subject to one of the most horrific genocides in recent world history. Survivors of such extreme situations of violence have traumatic memories of those events, memories that cannot be simply effaced or forgotten, but which also cannot be the sole basis for moving toward healing in a situation where the survivors have to continue to live together with the perpetrators. This is where poetry enters the scene—at first sight perhaps an unlikely candidate for overcoming trauma. But as she shows, in societies, such as those of Rwanda, in which a poetic tradition has long existed, that tradition itself is a profound means of structuring experience, making some kind of sense of it, and very importantly, expressing it. Furthermore, poetry releases creativity: it provides a form in which complex and terrifying experience can be embodied, shaped and communicated, and the discovery of this creativity in oneself is itself a major agency of healing and empowerment, and can indeed give rise to an "aesthetic of suffering"—a new way of expressing and transforming that suffering within an old form reshaped to contemporary needs (Grieder 2016: 42–46). In this sense she answers her own question: "How can poetry possibly contribute to healing the pain and suffering that have been caused by genocide?

What role can language—and poetry in particular—play in dealing with traumatic memories?" by showing that "poetic and metaphorical language is a way of coping with emotionally intense situations as it is a potent means of transcending pain and suffering" (Grieder 2014: 135). But while memory is by its very nature backward looking, it is also necessary to build hope for the future: "Expressing the inner world through the medium of words enables the individual to strike a balance between the memories generated by a painful past and the necessity for the self to exist in the present, the here and now (Grieder 2014: 136). The traditional African healer certainly uses herbs, stones and other material means, but also words—the "carriers of healing virtue", for in "reworking a text about the self, one also reshapes the self—a kind of interior sculpture", an open text that while it is never finished, is also the pursuit of an ideal of beauty—of relationships and an image of how the world should really be (Grieder 2014: 146–147).

This points the significance of narrative in two directions: as the healer of memories when those memories have been created through violence, and the cultural mechanism for the creation of new stories. The future, while certainly strongly shaped by the structures and attitudes inherited from the past, is never fixed or determined. Crucial to the quality of that future are the stories that we want and are able to create about it, a circumstance shaped primarily by the power of our imagination, a resource that is basically unlimited and inexhaustible. To create a just, sustainable and peaceful future is to first imagine it, then to embody it in the stories that we hear and teach, and then to realize it in practice. The beauty of the story is that it *is* the reality in a very real sense: the imaginative space in which what is created takes on its own powerful and experience shaping Being: the precondition for changes at any other level of society or culture to take place. Structural changes, while indeed, as history attests, while difficult to achieve do indeed happen. But the creation of new stories is within the capacity of many of us. Every society abounds in "space" where this can happen: songs, myths, poetry, utopias, visual art, music, ideas about nature, fantasy literature and science fiction, religions, folklore and local traditions, to say nothing of the potentially powerful transformative force of education, the media, psychotherapies, and such unlikely candidates as social, political and even economic theory. Cultures of violence are fueled constantly by the very media that we look to for guidance toward the future, and form and transmit values and conceptions of human relationships. Narratives, including those that come from the "edges" (the marginalized, the subaltern, the apparently voiceless) have power precisely because they create visions; hence the vital necessity of directing them toward the positive, the convivial and the socially and personally creative. In a very real sense, in our stories lies our salvation.

References

Arberry, A.J. (trans.). 1994. *Discourses of Rumi*. Richmond: Curzon Press.

Arendt, Hannah. 1958. *The Human Condition*. Chicago: University of Chicago Press.

Auden, W.H. 1972. *Selected Poems*, ed. Edward Mendelson. New York: Vintage.

Bax, Mart. 2004. Mass Graves, Stagnating Identification and War Violence in Rural Bosnia-Herzegovina. In Oscar Salemink, Anton van Harskaup, and Ananta Kumar Giri (eds.), *The Development of Religion/The Religion of Development*. Delft: Eburon.

Berry, Wendell. 2012. *New Collected Poems*. Berkeley: Counterpoint.

Boal, Augusto. 2008. *Theatre of the Oppressed*, trans. Charles A. and Maria-Odila Leal McBride and Emily Fryer. London: Pluto Press.

Bradley, James. 2017. Writing on the Precipice. *Sydney Review of Books*, February 21.

Brueggemann, Walter. 1988. *The Prophetic Imagination*. Philadelphia: Fortress Press.

Calvino, Italo. 1986. *The Uses of Literature*, trans. Patrick Creagh. New York: Harcourt Brace Jovanovich.

Clammer, John. 2012. *Culture, Development and Social Theory: Towards an Integrated Social Development*. London and New York: Zed Books.

Clammer, John. 2015a. *Art, Culture and International Development: Humanizing Social Transformation*. London and New York: Routledge.

Clammer, John. 2015b. Social Development and Peace. In *New Horizons of Human Development*, ed. A.K. Giri, 155–177. New Delhi: Studera Press.

Clammer, John. 2016. *Cultures of Transition and Sustainability*. New York and Basingstoke: Palgrave Macmillan.

Deming, Alison Hawthorne. 2001. *Writing the Sacred into the Real*. Minneapolis: Milkweed Editions.

Grieder, Andrea. 2014. Rwanda: Healing and the Aesthetics of Poetry. In *Arts and Aesthetics in a Globalizing World*, ed. Raminder Kaur and Parul Dave-Mukherji, 135–151. London and New Delhi: Bloomsbury Academic.

Grieder, Andrea. 2016. *Collines des milles souvenirs: Vivre apres et avec le genocide perpetre contre les Tutsi du Rwanda*. Geneva: Globethics.net.

Ghosh, Amitav. 2016. *The Great Derangement: Climate Change and the Unthinkable*. London and Gurgaon: Allen Lane.
Kleinman, Arthur, Veena Das, and Margaret Lock (eds.). 1997. *Social Suffering*. Berkeley: University of California Press.
Klein, Naomi. 2014. *This Changes Everything*. Harmondsworth: Penguin Books.
Korten, David C. 1999. *The Post-corporate World: Life After Capitalism*. West Hartford, CT and New York: Kumarian Press.
Korten, David C. 2006. *The Great Turning: From Empire to Earth Community*. San Francisco: Berrett-Koehler and New York: Kumarian Press.
McKibben, Bill. 1989. *The End of Nature*. New York: Anchor.
Meretoja, Hanna. 2018. *Storytelling and Ethics: Literature, Visual Arts and the Power of Narrative*. New York: Routledge.
Morris, David B. 1998. *Illness and Culture in the Postmodern Age*. Berkeley and London: University of California Press.
O'Sullivan, Edmund. 1999. *Transformative Learning: Educational Vision for the 21st Century*. London and New York: Zed Books.
Parales, Jon. 2014. Angelique Kidjo Puts a Continent on Her Musical Map. *International New York Times*, January 18–19, p. 17.
Paz, Octavio. 1990. *Alternating Current*, trans. Helen Lane. New York: Arcade Publishing.
Unger, Roberto Mangabeira. 2001. *False Necessity: Anti-necessitarian Social Theory in the Service of Radical Democracy*. London and New York: Verso.

CHAPTER 10

Advancing Cultural Rights: Holistic Development and Sustainable Futures

The argument of this book has proceeded along a number of parallel lines: that cultural rights are a necessary and natural extension of human rights; that the expansion of the notion of rights in this way greatly enriches the project of seeking holistic and just development; that what constitutes cultural rights needs to be expanded to include less discussed elements such as art and peace; and that the acceptance of the idea of cultural rights has a very positive feedback effect on the practice of culture and the nature of cultural expressions. Likewise, while the notion of justice has slowly expanded from a narrow legal definition to now include social and economic justice, so it needs to be extended even further into the realm of culture. Within culture itself, a holistic concept of justice needs to be extended beyond questions of access to cultural resources and protection of cultural diversity to include hitherto marginalized areas such as visual justice and the positive right to a clean, safe and attractive environment. Since culture is largely the product of the human imagination, this primary faculty needs to be directed to the remaking of society such that culture itself becomes a major tool for social transformation, a tool that transcends the pettiness and power-seeking of so much conventional politics. Cultural activism then becomes in a sense "the new politics"—a way of acting in and on the world beyond the truncated processes and institutions of "normal" politics, a form of human social activity that has not only failed dismally in addressing the large and pressing questions of our current planetary

J. Clammer, *Cultural Rights and Justice*,
https://doi.org/10.1007/978-981-13-2811-4_10

crisis, but has in many cases caused or fueled them. Clearly another model of social intervention is urgently required, and such an approach must be sought within culture.

Cultural rights themselves can be conceived along a number of dimensions—as entitlements, as capacities (and therefore in a sense potentialities rather than realized states), as resources (a huge repertoire of stories, myths, histories, paintings, buildings and so forth) that can be endlessly drawn on and recombined or added to in the creation of the next generation of cultural production, as "spaces" which allow exploration without any pre-given limits, and as responsibilities to use the given cultural heritage wisely and to create artifacts and expressions that both enhance and enrich the current generation while creating a legacy that will be passed to the next. The notion of responsibilities is a serious one, especially given the globalization of culture and the need to protect and transmit local cultures and languages and hence to maintain cultural diversity, and the fact that the world now faces a very uncertain future and unprecedented challenges. While these include the now tragically "normal" list of climate change, conflict, loss of biodiversity, pollution, deforestation, hyper-urbanization and the other usual suspects, it must also include the question of future cultures in a post-oil world and indeed in one of drastically reduced resources of all kinds including the most essential ones of water and clean air. This is taking place in a situation of an ever increasing global population and all the consequences that has for diminishing resources, food, living space, mobility, crime and in the bizarre situation of vast wealth concentrated in a few hands and a few countries, equally vast poverty and social exclusion and rising levels of inequality globally. An urgent need among cultural workers is to begin to address the question of what future sustainable cultures might be like and how we might achieve them. This necessarily involves questions of justice, not only the issues of aid and technical assistance or of taking steps to redress the structures created by and inherited from colonialism, but today also the fraught questions of responsibility for climate change, and for continuing access to diminishing resources, many, such as rare earths, vitally necessary for the technological gadgets which now dominate and in some cases quite literally control our over complex and machine-controlled societies.

Steps Towards the Future

How is this cultural reorientation toward the future to be achieved? Through a range of steps, the first of which is the recognition of cultural rights—the rights to expression, maintaining of language and lifestyles, the exercise of cultural agency and the recognition of the equality and value of all authentic cultures and the freedom to critique false, violent, demeaning, dehumanizing and anti-ecological ones. Such a basis provides the platform from which other modes of cultural action can be launched and expanded. Here I will suggest three primary means through which this can be done: the re-enchantment of the world, the education of desire and true sustainability.

Max Weber famously argued that the process of modernity, and its associated process of secularization, had brought about the "disenchantment" of the world: the loss of the dimensions of myth and fantasy that had animated the premodern world as we have progressively trapped ourselves in the "iron cage" of bureaucratic social organization and a culture of rationality that has seemingly driven out the non-rational (not, note, the irrational) from the realm of legitimate discourse. Insofar as this is true (and Weber did not discuss such significant areas as the sociology of the emotions or social psychology) it naturally suggests that the antidote to the managerial, bureaucratic and rationalized society is a good dose of re-enchantment. Some would suggest that this already happening as a spontaneous cultural response, signaled by the rise of fantasy literature and film, the highly significant reversal of secularization (although this is sadly often expressed in oppressive forms of fundamentalism) and the rise of interest in "spirituality" in its many possible forms including magic, yoga, some strands of the ecological movement, and the possible now largely defunct "New Age" movement and the large literature and many experiments in communal life that it engendered. Others would suggest that the process should be accelerated through whatever cultural mean are appropriate, including the encouragement of new and exploratory forms of spirituality, contemporary art, fantasy literature and science fiction, comparative religion, non-mechanistic approaches to nature, the foregrounding of the significance of the emotions in the understanding of culture, society and politics, and with it the body and the full range of sensory experiences which actually make up human's relationship with and reactions to the world (for example Stoller 1997). Matthew Del Nevo has suggested that enchantment is a human need, but one increasingly extirpated by the mass-culture industries, which, even when they appear to produce the desired product, actually only succeed in creating an ersatz version. While it might seem at first sight trivial, others too have argued for the active *re-enchantment* of both art as a major vehicle of the imagination (Gablik 2002) and of a wider engagement with other aspects of culture, including religion (Elkins and Morgan 2009).

How does all this connect to the idea of cultural justice? Essentially by "allowing" spaces of fantasy (and hence of imagination) free play, a process the outcome of which cannot be determined in advance, although may be channeled in socially progressive (understood as humanizing and ecologically sound) directions by encouraging and rewarding such endeavors. This contributes directly to the formation of the convivial society and the reconstitution of non-oppressive communities. Years ago, in his now classic work *Homo Ludens*, Jan Huizinga documented the ways in which play in its many forms is constitutive of human society and a necessary ingredient of social health (Huizinga 1970). The encouragement of play, and its close cousin humor, is an important form of what might be called joyful subversion—the undermining through fun, satire and non-bureaucratized leisure of the pretensions and joyless seriousness of most politics and economics. By re-enchantment, magic is indeed restored to the world, including the world of nature and its animal inhabitants, and with that process not only is beauty enhanced, but the desire to protect it is greatly increased. The pursuit of beauty can be a radical political act.

The second strand is the education of desire. Some human desires are clearly rooted in nature (biology)—the desire for satisfying foods including the love of both saltiness and sweetness, for sex during a substantial part of the life cycle, for companionship, for play and for an environment that pleases, which includes a strong aesthetic component. Many other "needs" however are socially manufactured—none of us need most of the things to be found on the shelves of a well-stocked supermarket, to drive around alone in a highly inefficient, resource consuming and pollution generating machine, to eat junk food, or to personally possess enough clothes to have satisfied an entire medieval village. Most addictions are socially manufactured—few if any arise from our basic nature. It follows from this that most consumption behavior is likewise manufactured, especially the forms of hyper-consumption that are so often exhibited whether as status seeking, identity forming or simply as addiction: no one really needs a thousand pairs of shoes or handbags, large collections of jewelry, multiple houses, several mobile phones, or for that matter a Picasso painting desired more for its enormous price tag than for either its aesthetic qualities or for its materials, since the latter consist simply of some oil paint applied to a piece of now aging canvas. Human society is full of such anomalies which have their roots in very odd systems of evaluation—that yesterday's rubbish can become today's antique, that we pay nurses scandalously less than men whose only visible skill is that of kicking a leather ball around a field for an hour and a half once or twice a week, that people who spend their time either impersonating other people or imaginary ones are called "stars", that house prices can be allowed to rise to extraordinary levels without the structures in question becoming in any way improved or expanded in situations where there is homelessness or where new entrants to the housing "market" cannot afford to buy even though they have quite respectable incomes.

The list could go on (and on), but the points that it illustrates are quite simple: that a just society requires the education and in many or most cases the diminution of our desires. In a crowded and increasingly resource poor world, and one in which the inhabitants of its richer parts consume far more than their proportional entitlement and produce far more pollution, trash and green-house gases, it is simply no longer responsible or acceptable to have large families. Small really is beautiful in that context. Related to this is the nature not just of our economic system, one driven by expansion, profit, resource extraction and consumption, but also of the economics that underpin it and which are transmitted in ever more abstract and often self-contradictory forms to each generation of economics students, but which is, as Carrier and Miller and collaborators have argued (1998), is really a "virtual" system—one which creates rather than describes the "reality" that it purports to report. Economy and culture are clearly intimately linked, and so cultural justice and economic justice are really inseparable, not only in the more obvious sense, but also in the perhaps more fundamental sense that we have allowed an anomalous situation to emerge in which economic values are largely allowed to trump cultural ones (just think of funding for the arts, or the proportion of international aid budgets that are devoted to culture) whereas, in a really sane society, it would be, and should be, exactly the other way around.

The education of desire then need not be some puritanical code of restrictions and shortages, but far more the achievement of abundance with the minimal use of resources, the minimal output of waste, "cradle to cradle" concepts and practice of design and manufacture, play and enjoyment, and the equable access to and distribution of the rewards: social, cultural, ecological and economic justice in other words. This throws considerable responsibility on the educational system: to educate for beauty, justice and responsibility, to enhance the social imagination and to direct creativity to humanizing ends.

This in turn connects, perhaps unexpectedly, with the search for true sustainability. Sustainability should not be thought of in purely survivalist terms—as somehow guaranteeing our future, a future of some kind—however minimalist. Rather sustainability should be thought of as the creation of a future society of abundance, different no doubt in radical ways from our current consumer driven, hierarchical and unequal version, but abundant in quality of life, conviviality, care for the less abled for any reason, and one based on restorative justice rather than the simple punishment of offenders. Its basis would then be respect for rights balanced with an equally strong sense of responsibility, sensitivity to the environment, the search for and creation of beauty in all sphere of life, including in architecture, design, urban planning, and the protection and nurturing of cultural diversity. This suggests a sociocultural future of more simplicity, in many ways "post-materialist", high levels of equality and genuine informed democracy, fulfilment of needs rather than wants, high levels of access to cultural resources and the encouragement of cultural expression by all age groups, genders, ethnicities and levels of physical and mental ability, and an education system that fosters such society-wide conviviality and community-building.

Culture is the deep grammar of any society. Its transformation then necessarily triggers fundamental changes in other levels of social, political, psychic and economic organization. More than one thinker has suggested that it is in the nature of human beings to be "world makers", whether imaginatively or in reality, or both, the one leading in many cases to the other. What is being built here is a new model, one that discerns a new set of relationships between aesthetics and politics, between culture and justice, between aesthetics and economics, and between cultural activism and transformative practice of other kinds. It sees social transformation as rooted in creativity and the social imagination. It recognizes cultural rights as a kind of applied ethics relating not so much to individual morality as an expanded version encompassing the environment, development, peace, the visual, design, and the actual expression of culture in making and in performance. Indeed, it is in this last category that much of the cultural innovation toward justice is taking place—in "design for the other 90%" (Smith 2007), in post-disaster architecture (Aquilino 2011), in film (Clammer 2015: 83–100), and very much in theatre, not only in the 'theatre of the oppressed' associated with the theatre activist and theoretician Augusto Boal (2008), but in many other forms of theatrical intervention in human rights issues, refugee situations, ecology, in community building, healing, and as providing the basis for a new aesthetics closely linked to social and political transformation (Fischer-Lichte 2008).

The question of aesthetics raises the broader question of the role of philosophical presuppositions in cultural analysis, and of the ways in which those presuppositions become the often unanalyzed basis for cultural assumptions. Our various civilizations are based on what might be thought of as "deep" assumptions—largely taken for granted world-views or cosmologies that structure everyday behavior. If, as suggested in this book, it is precisely our forms of civilization and their cultural practices—over consumption, prolific energy use, instrumentalist relationship with nature, extractive economies, addiction to violence—that have given rise to our planet-wide crisis, then it is in the nature of those civilizations and their reform to which we must also look for solutions. Many aspects of culture however do not lie on the surface, waiting to be easily discovered, rather they lie at those "deep" levels—our assumptions about nature, the body, time, gender, death and the future—that constitute the philosophical anthropologies from which we unwittingly operate, or which become manifest in such cultural formations as religions. Each form of politics, sociology or economics has its roots in some such epistemology and ontology—assumptions about the nature of knowledge and of Being. There are many who have argued that the roots of much of our planetary crisis can be traced to aspects of Western philosophy with its Cartesianism (the separation of mind and body), overemphasis on rationality, instrumentalism, preoccupation with analysis rather than synthesis or holism, and a conception of ethics, aesthetics and metaphysics as purely technical questions shorn of any dimension of mystery or enchantment. Such a view is usually rather essentialist and overdrawn, there being many alternative and oppositional strands in Western thought. But there are nevertheless important links of at least two kinds—Marx with his unacknowledged roots in his ancestral Judaism with its strong emphasis on social justice for example, as a benign example, but also the virtual hegemony of Western categories (democracy, progress, efficiency, development) over dominant ideas in politics, economics and social theory, a hegemony which the anthropologist Marshall Sahlins has masterfully deconstructed as being merely a form of local knowledge that for historical reasons (imperialism, early successes in technological innovation, exploration and resulting geographical knowledge) has become apparently universal (Sahlins 1996).

Many of the identity crises of modern life flow from cultural deprivation—from the denigration or marginalization of one's culture, its erosion or disappearance, its non-recognition. Reactions to this are varied—depression, resignation, fundamentalism, cultural nationalism, attempts to defend or revive the culture and/or language in question, seeking for an accommodation within some form of multiculturalism, or the evolution of new hybrid forms. The recognition of cultural rights goes a long way toward addressing many of these issues, and legitimates the protection of cultural diversity and the right of migrants (especially refugees) to reestablish their culture of origin in a new setting, while recognizing the reciprocal right of the host society to expect respect for its culture, and for some level of adaptation to its norms. Human rights should be as "large" as human beings in fact are—multifaceted and complex creatures with individual and collective histories, with memories, hopes and expectations, with traditions, religions and forms of inherited life, as well as an extraordinary capacity to adapt, change, evolve, survive, suffer, enjoy, celebrate and create new patterns of organization, expression and meaning. All of this is included within the elastic category of culture—the medium in which we swim as humans and which is the inescapable framework of our identities as individuals and as members of one or more communities, and increasingly of "virtual" ones too, spread across cyberspace and mediated by Facebook and its cousins. The recognition of the relationship between culture and justice is consequently a key to any humane and truly sustainable (and desirable) future.

This recognition also has implications for the nature of research in the social sciences in the light of these pressing planetary needs. A great deal of "research" is simply generated by the pressures of the academic promotion and ranking systems, and often has little social utility or imaginative interest, and indeed is rarely or never cited, except by its own authors. Research, however, in a situation of multiple global crises, should rather be directed at generating new facts and new insights relevant to finding solutions to those crises. Such research might have several characteristics. In their work on social movements in what they call the "age of austerity", Max Haiven and Alex Khasnabish propose the concept of "pre-figurative research"—research that is aimed not at discovering facts about the past, or even data about the present, but which "a research methodology that is borrowed from the future that we wish to create" (Haiven and Khasnabish 2014: 22). This summarizes their argument that today no research is neutral, but should be a vital part of the process of social transformation in which the fresh exercise of the imagination is essential. This suggests many fresh approaches to cultural research and research about culture, including the idea that many of the most interesting and original ideas come not from the cultural mainstream, but from the "borders", the areas or thinkers outside the canon, but fertile in their imaginative approaches. This may take many forms—what Linda Tuhiwai Smith has aptly called the "decolonization of methodologies" (Smith 1999), from listening to the cultural margins and to the poets and unrecognized thinkers who may well be producing the most original ideas, well below the radar of the academy, and from the recognition not only that conventional disciplinary boundaries are just that—conventional—but equally that it is at the boundaries of disciplines that new ideas arise. This provokes the exciting task of creating new epistemologies and categories of knowledge, recognizing that many established ones express in subtle ways existing hierarchies of power, gender and sectional interests. Given that culture itself is a dynamic process creative research has the potential to generate new models of interpretation, insight and application. Such research is of an "applied" nature given that it is concerned with not only what is, but creating knowledge that shapes the future, that future being the desirable one of sustainability and cultural justice.

The Western philosophical tradition however is obviously not the only one. One positive dimension of globalization is that it brings such thought systems into visibility and into contact with one another. They too demand to be listened to and to be taken seriously as authentic expressions of culture. If one turns to African philosophy (Eze 1997), or to the ancient Asian traditions, one finds such expressions in highly developed forms, spilling over into conceptions of ethics and aesthetics based on different assumptions about the world and human nature (or even, in the case of Buddhism, of whether there is one) and manifested in contrasting forms of visual culture and performance (Sasaki 2010). Such philosophical and cosmological "systems" are important for at least two reasons other than their intrinsic interest. The first is that they represent the "deep grammar" of their respective cultures. The other is that they too, as with Western patterns of civilization, need to be rethought in terms of how they, too, speak (or fail to) to our current planetary situation. While it is highly significant that virtually all major religious traditions are now rethinking their relationship to the environment, it is equally important that the philosophical anthropologies underpinning cultural formations be also interrogated in terms of their relationship to contemporary reality (Clammer 2013). Cultural justice, while as a concept is universal, in practice is always contextual—situated that is in relation to a particular culture and its history.

Asian philosophies and their associated religions (the two usually going together) face a paradoxical situation. On the one hand they have been criticized for lack of engagement with issues other than "interior" ones, but at the same time they offer radically alternative epistemologies to those found at the basis of most Western thinking. In many cases this gap is now being bridged by the emergence of socially engaged forms of Asian religions—very much so in Buddhism (Loy 2003; Jones 2003), but also in Islam (Engineer 2010), in Shinto, the indigenous religion of Japan (Clammer 2010), in Asian expressions of Christianity (Pieris 1992), and in Hinduism, where a number of thinkers working in the Advaita tradition have been concerned to link it to a concern with the world, not as illusion but as a very concrete reality, and to raise questions of ethics, freedom, liberation and confrontation with social and economic issues, drawing on the non-dual teachings of that form of philosophical and religious heritage (Rambachan 2006). The search for cultural rights and cultural justice must necessarily arise from the soil of actual cultures, not only at their surface levels, but also at their deeper ones. Those deep levels soon reveal, in every case, fundamental concern with ethics and with "correct" social relationships (something very marked in the Confucian tradition and the major influence that it has had on culture and social behavior in China, Korea, Japan and Vietnam). Cultural rights indeed might be seen as a contemporary expression of what in Buddhism are called "skillful means"—the best and fairest ways of achieving practical objectives through helping others, an ethics of compassion and the overcoming of enmities and the "three fires" of ignorance, ill-will and acquisitiveness, seen in classical Buddhism as the major barriers to achieving liberation. A culture of sustainability must also be one of cultural and social justice, and to move toward this requires not only a universal element, but also a "comparative" one in which the authenticity and epistemological and ontological validity of different cultures is fully acknowledged and celebrated, various paths toward liberation accepted as real alternatives, and practical (cultural and political work) steps to achieve cultural justice contextualized in the framework of cultural pluralism (Clammer 2018).

Cultures of Sustainability: Philosophical and Religious Sources

To creatively approach the future it is helpful to diagnose the present and the philosophical and ideological factors that have underpinned, if not caused, our current predicament. To find a path into that future a more expansive and imaginative model than the ones that have clearly failed, or at least outlived their usefulness, is needed: one that certainly involves critique of our current modes of thinking and practice, but which also embody visionary and creative (while realistic) suggestions for transformative action and thinking. It is in this context, and closely related to conceptions of rights, that an examination of the philosophical and religious roots of both our planet-wide crisis and possible solutions to it, must be sought. This is because our philosophies and religions are the source of the fundamental conceptions that shape our understanding of the world. These include our epistemologies—our theories of knowledge that structure that understanding, and our ontologies—our conceptions of Being in the world that shape our relationships both to one another and to all other entities that constitute our total environment. Every form of politics, sociology, anthropology or economics is, wittingly or not, underpinned by a philosophical anthropology.

Some have argued that our current global problems can be traced to significant aspects of Western philosophy with its emphasis on rationality, instrumentalism, the separation of mind and body, and analysis and reductionism rather than synthesis or holistic thinking. Such a picture can easily become a caricature, there being many alternative and oppositional strands in Western thought, some of which have had great impact, such as the Deep Ecology movement that has arisen from the work of the Norwegian philosopher Arne Naess. Certainly it is Western philosophy that has provided the basis for most contemporary political thought, whether Marxist, liberal or somewhere in between. But this philosophical tradition is not the only one, and in a globalized world in which cultures are brought into intimate contact with one another, so are systems of thought. As any notion of rights is rooted in a philosophical tradition of one kind or another, we should cultivate an interest in all such systems and ask the same critical questions that have been directed at the Western forms—notably, where do they too stand in relation to the planetary crisis that now confronts us?

For if Western philosophy has been, in many of its manifestations of an "applied" nature, this is on the whole less true of Asian philosophies with the notable exception of Confucianism. Can they, like the religious traditions with which they are mostly associated, be rethought as potentially valuable resources for addressing in creative ways our common problems? There are of course many issues here including that of searching for, in dos Souza Santos' words, alternative epistemologies from the South (Santos 2014), dialogue between "Eastern" and "Western" modes of thought, especially as they might apply to social theory, and exploring them not just from a textual scholars point of view, but as potential sources of creativity in building a new "practical philosophy" and philosophical anthropology that really speaks to the contemporary planetary situation. For it is only reasonable that they too should be interrogated as to their responsibility, even as Western philosophy and religion have been. For both are not simply cognitive systems, for they express or incorporate within themselves creativity and cultural imagination (indeed, perhaps *the* major expressions of these), forms of ethical imagination (new practices of relationship, attitudes toward nature, the creation or dissolving of social hierarchies, and the expansion of the scope of what we might include in the category of ethics itself—animals or beauty for instance) and, inevitably, visions of an alternative future. It has been persuasively argued that, for example, the Biblical book of Isaiah is one of the most socially radical texts ever written, and is utopian in the fullest sense of the word (Polak 1973). In the Indian context the writer and public intellectual Shiv Visvanathan has suggested that "Let us face it, the great reform movements of India were not the modernist, socialist or liberal democratic ones. The great reform movement was the bhakti tradition. Nanak, Kabir, Mirabai, did more to dent caste than *The Communist Manifesto*" (Visvanathan 2016: 31). This is important because it is tempting to focus primarily on the "grand" philosophies, forgetting the "minor" ones, when in fact vast storehouses of knowledge and wisdom are embodied in "indigenous knowledge", the long experience of tribal peoples, women, minorities of many kinds, who have in very many cases developed systems of knowledge and being-in-the-world that are both non-violent and sustainable in both ecological and sociological terms, and which embody insights into reality never conceived of by armchair academic philosophers (Berkes 2018; Subramanian and Pisupati 2010).

Asian philosophies have been criticized for lack of engagement with social issues, but yet at the same time they offer radically different epistemologies from those found at the basis of most Western thinking. But today an awareness of environmental crisis and social justice issues has impelled many of them to begin to examine their own theologies and practices and to rethink their relationship to today's great global issues, as well as the patterns of inequality (caste and gender in particular) that have been large parts of their traditional heritage. So within Buddhism has arisen the movement of "Engaged Buddhism"—applying Buddhist insights to such issues as the environment, peace and conflict resolution, gender and in particular the patriarchal structure of the *sangha* or monastic orders, human rights and wider issues that engage with capitalism, consumerism and politics (Jones 2003; Kaza and Kraft 2000; Loy 2003). In Hinduism, a number of writers have sought the environmental teachings embodied in the religion, and in Advaita in particular, quite successful attempts have been made to link it to a concern with the world, not as an illusion, but very much as a reality. This shift in emphasis poses questions of ethical behavior, freedom and liberation, and confrontation with social and economic issues, while raising the intriguing possibility of drawing on the non-dualistic teachings of the tradition. In this latter case Anantanand Rambachan has suggested that Advaita, with its philosophy of non-dualism, offers profound answers to what he calls the essential "human problem"—that we are intrinsically part of a larger unity, that we are in a metaphysical sense "incomplete" and tend to seek a sense of completeness through the pursuit of material possessions, status and power, things which must inevitably fail or come to an end (Rambachan 2006: 32–33).

Even Shinto, the indigenous religion of Japan, has undergone a similar transformation, and has attempted to repackage itself as a deeply ecological one (Clammer 2010). Christianity, which certainly has a good claim to be an Asian religion, has developed not only forms of "Liberation Theology" (initially in Latin America), but shaped this to the specificities of the Asian situation (Pieris 1992). Within Islam, a great deal of work has been done to identify and shape an Islamic economics and to engage directly with social justice issues through this, and through what, parallel to the terminology of Buddhism, is being called "Engaged Islam" (Engineer 2010). What we see then collectively is a fresh engagement of Asian, and in many parallel respects African philosophy with issues of social justice in general and the ecological crisis in particular. This is of profound importance because it signals not only a rereading of the traditions and scriptures of those various philosophical and religious traditions, but the emergence of what we might call a "methodology" for exploring issues of social philosophy, rights and responsibilities. For example, embodied in some such traditions, and in Buddhism in particular, is the recognition that suffering is intrinsic to being human, but also that such suffering can be largely overcome by the cessation of craving. The search for perfectability and its social expressions (Utopias in their various guises) through the adjustment of social, political and economic arrangements is illusory without confronting and uncovering what the Buddhist social activist scholar Ken Jones calls "institutional delusion"—the "three fires" of acquisitiveness, ill-will and ignorance—in which context he quotes the Indian sage Nagarjuna who speaks of the solution deriving from "revulsion from lusts, restraint from aggressions, vanity of possessions and power" (Jones 2003: 47). Such a position is underpinned by the assumption, certainly found in Buddhism and Hinduism, of the interconnected nature of reality, or of what the contemporary Buddhist thinker and activist Thich Nhat Hanh calls "inter-being". The recognition of this fundamental interdependency not only revolutionizes concepts of social justice (we are, if not all one, at least mutually dependent) and of rights (the pursuit of my rights can only be undertaken in the recognition of the equal validity of your rights, which cannot be violated by prioritizing mine).

All this is not to suggest another disguised form of cultural relativism. It is, to the contrary, to argue for the a priori validity of alternative forms of knowledge—what anthropologists might call "indigenous knowledge" and which de Sousa Santos calls "epistemologies from the South" and points to the process named by the Maori scholar Linda Tuhiwai Smith as the "decolonization of methodologies" (Smith 1999). Out of these arise not only alternative forms of knowledge, but also different framings of the idea of cultural rights, rooted in the specificities of each particular culture, while respecting the universalism of the principles enshrined in the UDHR. Worldviews are embodied in philosophies, which contain not only metaphysical expressions, but also ethical ones, and ethics writ large is social justice. The search for "liberation" undertaken through the medium of a philosophical/religious tradition need not only be conceived in individualistic terms, as personal enlightenment, but as an expression of "karma- yoga"—the identification and application of the "skillful means" through which positive and transformative effects may be made on the world as well (Paranjape 2005: 263). These means can take a variety of forms, and genuinely new ones when they arise from alternative epistemologies—expressed in practice as reexamining the whole concept of "management" (for example in the context of so-called "environmental management"), conceptions of leadership such as the emerging idea of "leadership for sustainability" (Parkin 2010) and the search for radically different economic principles and practices such as those embodied in "solidarity economy", degrowth theories, social economy, Islamic economics and other alternative forms (for a survey see Clammer 2016: 65–90). This all suggests a new and enlarged holistic paradigm in such fields as development studies (Schieffer and Lessem 2014) and social theory in general (Senge et al. 2005). Conceptions of cultural rights and cultural and social justice are enormously enriched by not only a "comparative" approach, valuable as that is, but by challenging the hegemony of certain Western philosophical ideas by acknowledging the variety and validity of very different philosophical and cultural systems, and by confronting and assimilating the other epistemologies and ontologies that anthropology and globalization have, between them, revealed to all of us.

Pursuing Cultural Rights/Seeking Integral Development

The uncovering of conceptions of cultural rights proves to be a rich and complex "anthropological" exercise—one that negotiates the global and the local, is concerned with the identification and recovery of forms of local knowledge, which respects the often radically differing epistemologies and aesthetics of different cultural systems, which seeks the preservation and protection of such systems in a dangerously culturally and linguistically homogenized world, which seeks not only to "respect" cultural rights to free expression, but to advance such rights and to establish their equality. The view of "development" being advanced here is clearly that not only is culture an essential element in any development discourse or practice, but that specifically cultural rights are an unavoidable component of any sustainable and desirable form of development, and certainly of any form that advertises itself as holistic or "integral".

Political activism is of course the main means by which people have sought to change society. The pursuit of cultural rights however, also entails cultural activism, which can take many forms. It can take the form of "arts activism"—the use of performance and other expressive means to confront, as has been done, such issues as globalization and the excesses of neo-liberal capitalism (and of the policing that underlies it—see Raunig 2007). It can also take the form of incorporating social justice issues into art education, and using art to promote social justice (Hanley et al. 2013), moving artistic and cultural interventions not merely to critique existing structures, institutions and inequalities, but to reconstruct them (Jackson 2011), recognizing the cultural dimensions of social movements, and working to protect and enhance forms of cultural production and expression, especially those in danger of erosion or suppression. Integral development must necessarily not only contain a cultural element—the minimalist "culture and development" position—but can be conceived of as *the development of culture*. This imposes a major task on the cultural worker—artist, critic, architect, academic, curator, arts administrator—to seek to create and promote truly authentic culture—work which promotes humanization, social justice, ecological responsibility, conviviality and beauty—and to oppose that which works against these goals and trivializes, divides and misrepresents. Cultural history is full of the latter, but the hour is too late for us to indulge in the false luxury of the unjust, the unsustainable and the dehumanizing, in whatever form these forces may take. Involvement in cultural activism for social and ecological justice is one of the great tasks of our time and participation in the "Great Work" of which the eco-theologian Thomas Berry speak (Berry 1999). For the seeking for rights, cultural and social justice and a rich and diverse natural environment is not something that can be left to politicians or economists, not only because of their failure to generate a holistic vision, but also because underpinning and flowing from political and economic initiatives are the cultural forms which give them shape, and out of which new patterns of culture and civilization must emerge if we are to have not only a future, but a vibrant and fulfilling one, not a minimalist existence, but one filled with creativity and imagination. For a politics (and economics) of the imagination is every bit as important as a politics of power and control, and more so, since it is ultimately the quality of our lives and our spaces of freedom and expression that make life worth living. "World making" in both reality and the imagination is perhaps the goal of human creativity, as certainly is hope, and clearly the pathway of any humane development, based firmly in rights, is to maximize the potential for that to happen, to everyone.

References

Aquilino, Marie J. (ed.). 2011. *Beyond Shelter: Architecture for Crisis*. London: Thames and Hudson.

Berkes, Fikret. 2018. *Sacred Ecology*, 4th ed. London and New York: Routledge.

Berry, Thomas. 1999. *The Great Work: Our Way into the Future*. New York: Bell Tower.

Boal, Augusto. 2008. *Theatre of the Oppressed*, trans. A. Charles McBride, Maria-Odilia Leal-McBride and Emily Fryer. London: Pluto Press.

Carrier, James G., and Daniel Miller. 1998. *Virtualism: A New Political Economy*. Oxford: Berg.

Clammer, John. 2010. Engaged Shinto: Ecology, Peace and Spiritualities of Nature in Indigenous and New Japanese Religions. In *Socially Engaged Religions*, ed. John Clammer, 50–61. Bangalore: Books for Change.

Clammer, John. 2013. The Project of Philosophical Anthropology. In *Philosophy and Anthropology: Border Crossings and Transformations*, ed. Ananta Kumar Giri and John Clammer, 21–38. London and New York: Anthem Press.

Clammer, John. 2015. *Art, Culture and International Development: Humanizing Social Transformation*. London and New York: Routledge.

Clammer, John. 2016. *Cultures of Transition and Sustainability*. Basingstoke and New York: Palgrave Macmillan.

Clammer, John. 2018. Towards Cultures of Sustainability: Interrogating and Renewing the Religious and Philosophical Sources of Our Planetary Crisis. In *Cultural Spaces for Sustainable Futures*, ed. Siddhartha, 212–228. Bangalore: Raindrop Publishers.

Elkins, James, and David Morgan (eds.). 2009. *Re-enchantment*. New York and London: Routledge.

Engineer, Asghar Ali. 2010. Engaged Islam. In *Socially Engaged Religions*, ed. John Clammer, 130–140. Bangalore: Books for Change.

Eze, Emmanuel Chukwundi (ed.). 1997. *Postcolonial African Philosophy: A Critical Reader*. Oxford: Blackwell.

Fischer-Lichte, Erika. 2008. *The Transformative Power of Performance: A New Aesthetics*. London and New York: Routledge.

Gablik, Suzi. 2002. *The Reenchantment of Art*. London and New York: Thames and Hudson.
Haiven, Max, and Alex Khasnabish. 2014. *The Radical Imagination: Social Movement Research in the Age of Austerity*. London and New York: Zed Books.
Hanley, Mary Stone, George W. Noblit, Gilda L. Sheppard, and Tom Barone (eds.). 2013. *Culturally Relevant Arts Education for Social Justice*. New York: Routledge.
Huizinga, Johan. 1970. *Homo Ludens: A Study of the Play Element in Culture*. London: Paladin.
Jackson, Shannon. 2011. *Social Works: Performing Art, Supporting Publics*. New York: Routledge.
Jones, Ken. 2003. *The New Social Face of Buddhism*. Boston: Wisdom Publications.
Kaza, Stephanie, and Kenneth Kraft. 2000. *Dharma Rain: Sources of Buddhist Environmentalism*. Boston and London: Shambhala.
Loy, David R. 2003. *The Great Awakening: A Buddhist Social Theory*. Boston: Wisdom Publications.
Paranjape, Makarand (ed.). 2003. *Dharma and Development: The Future of Survival*. New Delhi: Samvad India Foundation.
Parkin, Sarah. 2010. *The Positive Deviant: Sustainability Leadership in a Perverse World*. London and Washington, DC: Earthscan.
Pieris, Aloysius. 1992. *An Asian Theology of Liberation*. Maryknoll, NY: Orbis Books.
Polak, Fred. 1973. *The Image of the Future*. Amsterdam and New York: Elsevier.
Rambachan, Anantanand. 2006. *The Advaita Worldview: God, World, Humanity*. Albany: State University of New York Press.
Raunig, Gerald. 2007. *Art and Revolution: Transversal Activism in the Long Twentieth Century*, trans. Aileen Derieg. Los Angeles: Semiotext(e).
Sahlins, Marshall. 1996. The Sadness of Sweetness: The Native Anthropology of Western Cosmology. *Current Anthropology* 37 (3): 395–415.
Santos, Boaventuara dos Sousa. 2014. *Epistemologies from the South: Justice Against Epistemicide*. Boulder, CO: Paradigm Publishers.
Sasaki, Ken-ichi (ed.). 2010. *Asian Aesthetics*. Singapore and Kyoto: National University of Singapore Press and Kyoto University Press.
Schieffer, Alexander, and Ronnie Lessem. 2014. *Integral Development: Realizing the Transformative Potential of Individuals, Organizations and Societies*. Farnham and Burlington, VT: Gower.
Senge, Peter C., Otto Scharmer, Joseph Jaworski, and Betty Sue Flowers. 2005. *Presence: An Exploration of Profound Change in People, Organizations and Society*. New York: Doubleday.

Smith, Cynthia E. 2007. *Design for the Other 90%*. New York: Cooper-Hewitt National Design Museum.

Smith, Linda Tuhiwai. 1999. *Decolonizing Methodologies: Research and Indigenous Peoples*. London and New York: Zed Books.

Stoller, Paul. 1997. *Sensuous Scholarship*. Philadelphia: University of Philadelphia Press.

Subramanian, Suneetha, and Balakrishna Pisupati (eds.). 2010. *Traditional Knowledge in Policy and Practice: Approaches to Development and Human Well-Being*. Tokyo: United Nations University Press.

Visvanathan, Shiv. 2016. *Theatres of Democracy: Between the Epic and the Everyday*, ed. Chandran Gowda. Noida: HarperCollins.

Index

J. Clammer, *Cultural Rights and Justice*,
https://doi.org/10.1007/978-981-13-2811-4

The manufacturer's authorised representative in the EU is Springer Nature Customer Service Centre GmbH, Europaplatz 3, 69115 Heidelberg, Germany. If you have any concerns regarding our products, please contact ProductSafety@springernature.com

Printed and bound by CPI Group (UK) Ltd, Croydon, CR0 4YY
25/09/2026
02222897-0001